Creative Ideas for Worship with All Abilities

Creative Ideas for Worship with All Abilities

Hazel Bradley
and
Jim Cargin

CANTERBURY
PRESS

© Hazel Bradley and Jim Cargin 2019

First published in 2019 by the Canterbury Press Norwich
Editorial office
3rd Floor, Invicta House
108–114 Golden Lane
London EC1Y 0TG, UK
www.canterburypress.co.uk

Canterbury Press is an imprint of Hymns Ancient & Modern Ltd
(a registered charity)

Hymns Ancient & Modern® is a registered trademark of
Hymns Ancient & Modern Ltd
13A Hellesdon Park Road, Norwich,
Norfolk NR6 5DR, UK

British Library Cataloguing in Publication data

A catalogue record for this book is available
from the British Library

978 1 84825 119 3

Typeset by Regent Typesetting Ltd

We dedicate this book in deep gratitude to two people who have,
through their courage and resilience
in the face of deepening physical weakness,
inspired us throughout this project: Emily and Pauline.

Contents

List of illustrations

The publisher and authors acknowledge with thanks permission to use copyright owners' photographs and illustrations. Every effort has been made to contact the sources and we would be grateful to be informed of any omissions. Wikimedia Commons images are used by a Creative Commons Attributions-ShareAlike 3.0 licence.

Part 4: How to plan creative inclusive small group celebrations

Appendix 5: Templates

Acknowledgements

We gratefully acknowledge the wise advice of many, many people in the writing of this book, including those listed below, but any responsibility for errors remains with the authors. We are certainly grateful for their practical contribution, but their ongoing encouragement has been just as important.

We would also like to thank our families, and the L'Arche communities which we are part of, in London and Brecon.

We are indebted to our commissioning editor, Christine Smith, for her patience and guidance to us as new authors, to Mary Matthews for her tireless search for engaging images, and the whole editorial team at Canterbury Press for making this book a reality.

All the Bible passages have been adapted and sometimes abridged by the authors.

Artists

Revd Ally Barrett at: https://reverendally.org/art/
Revd Adam Boulter at: www.adamboulter.co.uk
Katharine Hall at: www.davidebutler.co.uk
Thomas Lacroix at: www.spanglefish.com/thomaslacroixarts/index.asp
Sylvia Lear
Le Pot-en-Ciel studio of L'Arche Beloeil: Harold Lejeune in collaboration with Élisabeth Eudes-Pascal (http://z-e-p.blogspot.com)
Revd Cécile Schnyder
Moe Suzuki
Masaichi Wakamoto

For permission to use their artwork we thank:
L'Arche Trosly for the Icon of the Presentation, Artisanat des Monastères de Bethléem
St Beuno's for the painting of the Visitation by Claudia Williams
Faith and Light International for the Icon of the Crucifixion
The Community of Grandchamp for the Icon of Jesus appearing to Mary Magdalene:
Assiya Peter d'Cruz

Veronica Linehan
Fr David Meyrick
Katarzyna Mierzwiak
Antonio Pacitti
Muneshwar Yadav
Philip Yates

All the pictures in the book may be downloaded for free in larger sizes and in colour from the Canterbury Press website, at www.canterburypress.co.uk

Song writers

John Coleman at: johncoleman.bandcamp.com
Brian Halferty
Rowland Howarth
Peter Kearney at: peterkearneysongs.com.au (for giving permission for the melody and lyrics of 'Come Now Holy Spirit')

Photographers

Hazel Bradley
Dorothee Giedroyc
Raimonda Sidaraite

Consultants

We thank those who have participated in celebrations led by L'Arche at Greenbelt or in other places. Many of these ideas are used in this book.

We have greatly appreciated the moral support, advice and input of the following: Hilary Lacroix, Revd David Stephenson and other members of L'Arche UK's National Reflection Council, as well as Fr Mark Beattie, Lal Keenan, Revd Gill O'Neill and Robin Yates.

We are grateful to the Revd Peter Cole for his permission to use his Holy Communion Prayer.

Louise Carter, Fr Chris Hughes and Maria Noonan deserve a special mention for their endless availability, countless wise suggestions and sheer fun to work with.

We owe a special debt of gratitude to the 'Pray-ers': The Benedictine sisters at Minster Abbey, Kent and the sisters of the Society of the Sacred Cross at Tymawr Convent, near Monmouth and the church leaders who accompany L'Arche in the UK:

Revd Steve Butler, Scottish Episcopal Church
Bishop Stephen Conway, the Anglican Communion
Fr Jock Dalrymple, Roman Catholic Church in Scotland
Bishop Nicholas Hudson, Roman Catholic Church in England and Wales
Revd John Gillibrand, Anglican Church in Wales
Revd Fiona Smith, Church of Scotland
Revd Gerry Stanton, Baptist Minister
Bishop Mark Strange, Primus of the Scottish Episcopal Church

Donors

This work was undertaken by L'Arche and was funded, in part, by the Sir Halley Stewart Trust. The views expressed are those of the authors and not necessarily the trust. Further financial support came from another donor who wishes to remain anonymous.

Foreword

by the Rt Revd Stephen Conway

In June 2017, I had the privilege to participate in the inclusive celebration, worship and communal consultation which was the international meeting of delegates of l'Arche communities from around the world. This happens every five years and I was there as one of the church representatives. Each day I was one of the players in the very participative and visual offering of the worship. The inclusive team was made up of people with learning disabilities, assistants and an awkward bishop. The whole gathering that week experienced and lived both the principles and the opportunities offered by this book.

Hazel and Jim set out five clear principles and provide a helpful questionnaire for churches to enable a wider network of worshipping communities to reflect health-ily exactly how inclusive they really are as opposed to how they think they may be. It is a positive book which does not bemoan the obstacles to the inclusion of every child of God, whatever their abilities, but rather illustrates from real examples what true welcome looks like.

The book provides excellent materials for worship which are not meant to entertain or occupy but to lead all of us into profound depth through wide partici-pation in dramatic engagement with the Bible and shared celebration and joy in Christ. The book, therefore, practises what it preaches very accessibly. It responds to the truth of research undertaken with people with learning disabilities who say, sign and express that they love coming to church, but wish sometimes that they were invited to engage and lead at a deeper level as disciples, commissioned by the baptism that shapes us together as the Body of Christ.

This excellent resource and challenge to our thinking helps me to reflect on the prepositions we use in developing ever more inclusive belonging through our worship. We do not provide opportunities for people and just give to them. We celebrate with people who show some vulnerability so that we can discover all the beauty in the humanity we share. We have so much to gain from people who often teach us to love.

+ *Stephen Conway*
Bishop of Ely

Bishop Stephen Conway serves as the official Anglican representative on the ecumenical group of church leaders who accompany L'Arche International, a role he fulfils alongside representatives of the Roman Catholic and Protestant churches.

Preface

The purpose of this book

'All of us are welcome and all of us is welcome.' A Parish Council meeting of All Saints Church, West Dulwich, London, fastened on this thought-provoking phrase as a neat way of highlighting the impact of people with learning disabilities on their church. Several members of the local L'Arche community are active members of this parish, among others welcomed with a learning disability. *'All of us are welcome and all of us is welcome.'* Meaning?

The first part is pretty straightforward: contrary to any mistaken idea that the church is only for certain types of people, *'all of us are welcome'* flags up that the church welcomes anyone seeking to follow Jesus, irrespective of disability or any other possible bar.

But *'all of us is welcome'*? This needs unpacking. The experience of All Saints is that because people with a learning disability are made to feel welcome, this encourages other church members to bring their own vulnerability. In other words, going to church doesn't mean leaving the 'messy bits' at the door. Jesus welcomes the whole of our humanity: not just what we are most proud of, but our places of weakness, embarrassment. An example may help: some parents with young children at All Saints consistently report that the presence of people with learning disabilities encourages them when their own children and babies are noisy. This is not because the L'Arche folk make a lot of noise (!), but rather that their presence is a sign that this is a church that welcomes each person in their full humanity. In this light, the person with a disability is helping the congregation to fulfil its mission. So, inclusion works both ways: the individual person with a learning disability certainly benefits, but so does the whole congregation. This is very much the spirit in which we offer this book.

Introduction

This book is grounded in our conviction that when a church becomes more inclusive, it more faithfully represents the body of Christ. Seen this way, inclusion is not about doing something extra, but about enabling a church to realize its own identity more fully, and so carry out Christ's mission to share the gospel more effectively.

With that in mind, Parts 1 and 2 offer a range of know-how which we ourselves have used, or seen used, to support a person with a learning disability to participate fully in the life of their church community. In Part 3, the reader will find 12 inclusive church services. Readers might like to turn to this section first, trying to imagine how these examples might work in their own church. Be creative! The tools and ideas outlined in Parts 1 and 2 are intended to help you mix and match, adapting as needed to make a better fit to your own situation. In Part 4, given that small prayer groups play an important part in the life of many churches, we offer some guidelines for planning small group celebrations and then 12 sample celebrations for small groups to use and adapt. Finally, the Appendixes make available a range of other useful resources.

We have, where possible, included many diverse real life examples of good practice. This shows that thankfully, far from being an untried theory, inclusion is very much a lived practice, helping congregations week in and week out, in both their worship and witness. Indeed, more and more churches today up and down the UK are discovering the many-sided ministry of men, women and children with learning disabilities.

A word about L'Arche

Many of the examples in this book draw on the experience of L'Arche in the UK and beyond. L'Arche is an international federation now comprising over

150 communities, spread across 38 countries throughout the world: it offers life opportunities to all its members, who include men and women with learning disabilities, their friends and carers. L'Arche was founded in France in 1964 by Canadian philosopher, Jean Vanier and two men with learning disabilities, Raphael Simi and Philippe Seux.

In Vanier's vision (www.jean-vanier.org), what has guided the work of L'Arche from the start has been the conviction that each person is a potential source of life, with something unique and valuable to contribute to their circle, their neighbourhood and to wider society. L'Arche aims to unlock each person's potential, through a combination of excellent professional skills, and an attitude of warm acceptance. It is rooted in the belief that each human being is on a spiritual quest to find meaning in their life; while each person's path is uniquely their own, we can still share the journey together: the important thing is to encourage each other's personal development, and celebrate the gifts and talents that emerge.

There are 12 L'Arche communities in the UK (www.larche.org.uk for more details), and each has experience of supporting men and women with learning disabilities who wish to participate in the life of their local church.

A word about terminology

There is no universally agreed vocabulary to describe the condition which we in this book are calling learning disabilities. The World Health Organization uses the term 'intellectual disabilities'. Others prefer 'learning difficulty'. We have opted for 'learning disabilities' and 'learning disability' as these are probably the most widely used terms today in the UK, where this book is being published.

Delighting in the gifts of all our members

Five basic principles have guided our thinking in writing this book:

- Each Christian, by virtue of their baptism, has been incorporated into Christ's body and so shares in his mission of peace to the world.
- Disability of any kind, far from inhibiting the church from fulfilling Jesus' mission, in fact enables the church to better represent Jesus and his message in the world.
- The church's intention is to help each member fully to live out their vocation.
- Jesus said, 'the Sabbath is made for humanity': so too the church service.
- Inclusion is not a once-and-for-all phenomenon, but a work in progress.

St Paul: prophet of inclusion

If the church is to be truly whole, then everyone needs to be welcomed, and the 'vulnerable' need to be at its heart. Many modern prophets in the church, including Jean Vanier, founder of L'Arche, insist that the church cannot be truly whole unless the 'poor' are invited to the centre. The vulnerable are those pushed to the margins for a variety of reasons including disability. Inclusion is the popular current term for involving people, but as a description, it is really rather weak: this book prefers to speak about belonging, as described by Jean Vanier and John Swinton:

> The friendship that is given to us in Jesus calls us to move beyond mere inclusion towards belonging. To belong, you need to be missed. To belong, others need to long for you like the prodigal son's father as he anxiously surveys the horizon, searching eagerly for signs of his son … To belong we need to feel that we matter. Belonging is the true place of meeting.[1]

Vanier and Swinton are, in fact, advocating for the place of people with a psychiatric illness in the church, but exactly the same argument applies to others on the margins, including men and women with learning disabilities. The point is to *welcome* vulnerable people to the centre, and really *celebrate* each person's presence, gifts and talents, and create a culture where each person knows that they can come just as they are.

It is vital to recognize from the 'get-go' that this approach has nothing to do with any kind of favour, or well-meaning act of generosity: on the contrary, it is, rather, a simple recognition that without their full participation, the church's own mission is seriously handicapped. Vanier and Swinton again: 'Only when we can come to realize that the Church cannot be the Church without each member of the body feeling that they belong, can we truly be the Church.'

When you belong, you feel at home. When Sylvia was asked to draw her church she drew the home she always drew, then added a cross on top. Can we make our churches places where all people belong and are at home?

Encouragingly, there is really nothing new in this cry: right from the start, St Paul likened the church to the human body. In his first letter to the church in Corinth, Paul recognizes that each member of the body has a particular and vital role to play. If one person is excluded, then it really does matter as the body depends on each part.

Notably, Paul claims that the weakest parts of the body deserve special honour. In relation to church members with a disability, such honour is sometimes interpreted as a need to provide a special annual service. But the reader will not find the resources for such a service in this book. This is intentional. Our point is that such special services, however well intended, can become tokenistic, actually running counter to real inclusion. Instead of truly enabling the person with a disability to participate in the regular weekly life of the parish, these services can unintentionally keep them at a distance. Real belonging happens day by day, week by week, which is also how the congregation will benefit from the gifts and presence of a person with a disability in their midst.

Inclusion helps the church

So what does inclusion add to the church? Revd Clare Herbert shares her own perceptions, based on her experience as an assistant priest in All Saints. At the point of moving house, she spoke in her final sermon of the quite unexpected gift of people with learning disabilities in the congregation, most but not all of whom came from the nearby L'Arche community:

> I want to thank the L'Arche community for their presence here. I have struggled with why this presence has become so very important to me and why it has left such a deep imprint when I have not had time to become involved, as many of you are. I think it is because L'Arche folk help me enter more honestly into what it is to be human without guile or pretence around this altar. When Patrick sitting near me, has cried out, 'Fish and chips!' continually throughout someone's lengthy sermon, I have giggled because I too have been thinking of getting home more than about what's being said. When Maggie has shouted, 'Hello! I'm here!', I have recognized the Clare who sometimes comes into church desperately wanting someone to say my name and give me a hug, but am far too inhibited to say so.

And Clare concludes: 'L'Arche has deepened for me the experience of what it is to be a human community before God in humility and truth – no, not before God, *with* God.' '*A human community*' echoes Paul again, writing this time to the Galatians:

> All of you are children of God, through faith, in Christ Jesus, since every one of you that has been baptised has been clothed in Christ. There can be neither Jew nor Greek, there can be neither slave nor free, there can be neither male nor female – for you are all one in Christ Jesus. (Galatians 3.26–28, NJB)

And in the same vein, neither is there disabled nor non-disabled.

Getting to know you

One trap to avoid is grouping: no one wants just to be seen as a member of 'the disabled group'. Each of us wants to be seen and appreciated for the unique individual that God made us to be. Each person does belong to various groups and, clearly, these play an important part in our lives, but at the end of the day, God calls each person by name. By the same token, it is only in getting to know a person as an individual that they trust enough to reveal their gifts and preferences as well as their limitations, those areas needing a particular support or care. This is the first step to finding a suitable ministry. For instance, a particular person with a learning disability might struggle to read the lectionary, but be brilliant at welcoming people into the church and giving them their hymnbook. Each ministry or role requires a different skill-set; some are more high-profile, others less so. But when all these ministries work in harmony together, they bear witness to how a Christian community can fulfil its mission in Christ.

Henri and Janet's mutual blessing

This point about confirming each other's ministry is well-illustrated by the experience of Henri Nouwen, the well-known spiritual writer and speaker. Henri lived the last years of his life in the L'Arche community of Daybreak in Ontario, Canada. Before coming to L'Arche, he had been a highly regarded university professor and attracted a wide following through his many books and talks. In spite of his success, Henri sensed something was missing in his life: he simply needed to slow down. Easier said than done, given the constant requests and suggestions for new projects he received. So he arrived in Daybreak, and started getting to know the intellectually disabled members of the community. It was a revelation to him. Henri discovered that a disabled person could give him exactly what he needed: permission to slow down, by calling him to be present just to the person in front of him. One episode in particular stands out, the day that Janet Munro, a woman with learning disabilities, taught him a lesson in slowing down and being present:

> As he was walking into the chapel to celebrate the Eucharist, Janet stopped Henri. 'I want you to give me a blessing,' she said. Without thinking much about it, Henri responded, 'Janet, God bless you in the name of the Father, the Son and the Holy Spirit.' 'Oh no!' said Janet, 'That is not good enough. I want a real blessing.' Henri, taken aback, apologized and asked Janet to wait until the end of the Eucharistic celebration.
>
> When Mass was over, Henri said to the group, 'Before this celebration, Janet asked me for a blessing. I was in a hurry then, but now I am ready. So, Janet could you come forward?' Henri held out his arms, and Janet walked right up to him so that her head was close to his chest. He gently laid his hands on her head and said, 'Janet, God has made you into such a beautiful woman, and I believe that God loves you very dearly. God wants you to know that you are a wonderful person, and God wants you to continue to be a loving person in your family and in the community and beyond. Go now, and remember that you are loved and that you have the gift of love to give to others.'
>
> Janet turned to sit down and almost at once Mary Anne said, 'What about me? I want a blessing too!' When she turned to go, Greg was there, followed by Patsy, Karen, Julie, Kim, John and many others.[2]

And that was how Henri blessed Janet. Like all blessings, it brought her new life. But it could justifiably be called the story of Janet's blessing. For wasn't Janet also blessing Henri, in her own way, simply by asking him for a blessing? Her blessing was less obvious perhaps and for that reason easy to overlook altogether, but Janet certainly brought Henri new life, that day.

All of the pictures in the book may be downloaded for free in larger sizes and in colour from the Canterbury Press website, at www.canterburypress.co.uk.

Welcome to our church:
Bridges and obstacles

Before naming some of the obstacles that can confront people with learning disabilities in churches, let's look at some instances of a 'good welcome'. For instance, Tommy, by reason of his autism, always needs to sit in the same place at the front of the church, and this is well known by his church. So, when a visitor sits in Tommy's place unaware, another member of the congregation will gently suggest they sit elsewhere. This is a way of supporting Tommy in his needs. Similarly, Celia, a member of the congregation, always made sure that she was near Simone, a church member with a learning disability, in order discreetly to help her through the service. And if you asked Celia about this, she would tell you about the ways in which she herself gets support from Simone in her vocation as a Christian wife and mother. In another church, Christine's congregation has got used to her turning round to wave to her friends, and smiling at everyone else, especially children and babies! For her, communion is about relationship. It is acceptance like this that makes the church more welcoming not just for the 'Christines' of the world, but for all comers. Similarly, Patrick managed to open up his church by cheerfully greeting everyone possible at the sign of peace: from being a rather stiff formal church, it became a congregation much more at ease with itself. It is as if Patrick was sent by the Holy Spirit to bring a deeper unity, breaking down unnecessary barriers between people. When Paul could no longer endure a long sermon at a mass for the final vows of a Jesuit, his voice rang out loud and clear, 'Amen!', giving a not too subtle hint to the preacher! Many people thanked Paul afterwards! It was the part of the sermon that was most remembered! His sheer honesty was maybe admired, and even envied!

All of these are instances of a church acting as a warm and welcoming community. Unfortunately, it does not always happen like that! Sadly, a congregation sometimes simply does not know how to respond to a person with a learning disability in their midst: making no allowances, giving no extra support to include the person. And first appearances really do count. If a person does not feel welcomed the first time that they pluck up courage and come into a particular church, then why would they come back for a second dose? It is worth noting that a lack of welcome doesn't often show itself in outright unfriendliness, like glaring at someone for making distracting noises, or refusing to shake a person's hand at the sign of peace. More often, it can be more complicated than that: some congregation members can try so hard to be 'Christian' that they unconsciously adopt a patronizing attitude towards a person with learning disabilities, treating them as a child, or 'a poor unfortunate', rather than in a way appropriate to their age, whether child, teenager or adult. However well intended, this approach too is far removed from a genuine spirit of welcome.

There can also be a kind of institutional exclusion: this is when the attitude of the church itself unconsciously excludes people with learning disabilities. For instance, services can sometimes become over-formalized, attempting to perform the ritual to perfection. In such a scenario, where is the place of a person with a learning disability such as Bob who cannot be quiet through a whole service? Is Bob just a nuisance, spoiling the ritual and disturbing the peace? But what if he is a messenger from God, sent to remind us of Jesus' words: 'the Sabbath is made for humanity!' Put another way, the person with a learning disability can give permission to each person to bring their whole humanity to church, not just the presentable or acceptable parts. This is not to argue against a certain formality: there are clear advantages when the congregation knows what is happening next. It is more a reminder that a church service is less about creating a perfect performance and more about enabling each person to participate as a member of God's family. In the example above, the priest makes a point of greeting Bob by name at the start of the service, modelling a welcoming attitude by his own example.

Physical barriers should not need to be mentioned these days, but it is sadly still true that lack of access to, or within, the church building remains an issue in some churches. In assessing the reasonable modifications that the law requires, it can be really helpful for a church working party to include a few people with accessibility issues: whether to do with hearing, seeing, moving about, or understanding, it is so easy for the 'temporarily able-bodied' among us to have blind spots. Wouldn't it be wonderful for all the churches in a locality to be well known for their welcome of all kinds of people?

Lengthy, intellectual sermons can also convey a subtle message that only certain types of people are wanted in a particular church: 'If you don't understand, then maybe you are better off looking elsewhere for your spiritual needs.' And yet, Jesus showed that simple stories about characters one can identify with have a universal appeal and get the key message across in a memorable way. In our times as much as his, however, there can be a tendency for the church to act like a club for the elite, rather than a community for the broken, lost and searching people of God. In such an exclusive club, the person with a learning disability is judged negatively for not understanding at an intellectual level, as if faith were dependent on intelligence.

In giving retreats, Jean Vanier often tells the story of a young person with learning disabilities who was making his first holy communion. At the end of the service his uncle said to the boy's mother, 'Such a beautiful service! What a pity he understood nothing.' The mother's eyes welled up in tears. But her son said to her, 'Never mind Mummy. Jesus loves me just as I am.' This points to one of the gifts that a person with a learning disability can bring to a church: helping it to focus on the essentials of faith, on each believer's relationship with Jesus.

PART 1

Towards an inclusive church:
How to include people with a learning
disability in the life of the church

A questionnaire on disability and inclusion for a church leadership team

This questionnaire aims to encourage greater awareness of disability. In filling in this form, it would be helpful to consult individuals with disabilities in the church, and where needed, their friends and/or support workers. (The form may be downloaded free of charge from the Canterbury Press website: www.canterburypress. co.uk).

How does disability and learning disability fit with our theological outlook?

What difference would it make if people with learning disabilities were not here?

How can we make sure that adults with learning disabilities are fully welcomed and included in the life of our church?

Before the service?

During the service? *Think about participation/language/choreography and movement*

After the service?

Between Sundays?

What are the particular gifts and ministries of the individual people with learning disabilities in our church?

How can we better enable those people to exercise their gifts and ministries?

Is our welcome genuinely inclusive, or simply tokenistic?

Examples of specific ministries including people with learning disabilities

Through baptism, a human being is recognized as a member of God's family. The Holy Spirit pours out plentiful gifts on each, so that they can serve Christ's mission in a way suited to their unique mix of strengths and weaknesses, be they of body, mind or spirit. In order to discover a person's gift, it is vital to get to know them as an individual. This is as true for a person with a learning disability as it is for anyone else.

When it comes to church services, many people with learning disabilities can join in with most things that happen, and love to be given an opportunity. Each example below shows how this can work in practice. While some can accomplish their ministry independently, others may need prompting, to a greater or lesser extent. But the fact that someone needs extra support should not be considered a disadvantage. On the contrary, this gives a clear message to the congregation and visitors, that 'we are a church where ministry is something shared by many; a church where we support each other to bring forth our gifts; and this is nothing exceptional, but part and parcel of our life in Christ'.

Here are some practical ways that people with learning disabilities can contribute to a church service: the lesson is that small allowances and discreet support can make a big difference.

Bell-ringing   In some churches, a person with a learning disability is on the bell-ringing team, summoning the congregation to worship.

Welcoming   Giving out service sheets and hymnbooks as people arrive. Worshippers at one church pick up their service sheets from the tray on Michael's wheelchair. It usually takes Michael time to respond to a question, which means others need to slow down and listen carefully – not a bad preparation for the church service! At another church, Diana is proud to put on her name badge, showing she is a member of the welcoming team, a role she performs with great enthusiasm.

Serving   Ralph is proud to be on the team of servers and is sometimes invited to carry the processional cross. When this happens, he is given a lighter cross, for the sake of safety – an example followed by some other team members as well. In another church, Jennifer is always paired with someone able to give her a supporting hand on the steps to the altar.

Singing and playing music   Daniel, blessed with a good sense of rhythm, is much appreciated for his drum-playing in his church. Sandra, who is blind, taught herself to play the piano by ear and uses that gift in her church. Karen joined her church's music group once someone had spotted her talent at the guitar. Tuning is something she cannot manage on her own, so another member of the group does that for her each week.

Reading   Instead of breaking open God's word in the same way each week, why not invite a group of people with and without learning disabilities to mime it now and then? This happens in some churches, and can bring new insights to a familiar Gospel passage.

Taking up the collection   A long time ago, Christine's priest took the inspired decision to invite her to take up the collection each week, a service she has now performed faithfully for many years. Now that she needs more support to fulfil this ministry, she does it in company with another person, who goes first to Christine: then one greets, while the other passes the plate. Christine takes the collection up to the altar on her own, giving it to the priest or deacon (not infrequently with a kiss!), before making a deep liturgical bow and returning smiling to her place. For many, this is a highlight of the service!

Reading the intercessions   A person with learning disabilities could read a prayer, or say a prayer spontaneously, or lead a refrain such as, 'Lord in your mercy' or 'Amen'. Depending on a person's confidence and ability, they might need to do this as one of a pair.

Ministering the consecrated bread and wine at the time of communion   There is no reason, why, with training and support, a person with a learning disability could not fulfil this important ministry with the required reverence and care.

What about collecting hymnbooks and service sheets at the end of the service? Sophia began doing this on her own initiative, her in-built desire for order meaning that she makes a good job of stacking the hymn books.

Helping with tea and coffee after the service   Some people are exceptionally good at welcoming others, and really come into their own with a ministry like this.

These are just some of the named ministries needed during a service. Outside the service itself, churches need cleaning, the sick need visiting and raffle prizes need wrapping ... the list goes on. For churches with a Parish Council, why not consider including a person with a learning disability? If one just starts by asking 'why not?' rather than 'why?' the person with a disability can be appreciated as someone called to serve the church as much as any other member, with their varied gifts and talents. Seen in this light, it is not really such a big deal if a particular person needs a little extra support. As each takes their rightful place in the body of Christ, the church will increasingly be understood as an open community for the many, rather than a closed club for the few.

Guidelines on accompanying a person with learning disabilities to church

This could accompany the Church Belonging Form on pp. 12–14 in a person with learning disabilities' care plan.

How to support a person with learning disabilities to attend Sunday services at their church? Here are some pointers for their caregivers. When the person is a regular, known and loved member of the congregation, you already have a head start. But help may be needed to support a person with learning disabilities to choose which church they wish to become a member of and attend. This could involve attending several churches for their Sunday worship, before deciding which one suits best, according to a range of factors including proximity, ease of access, style of worship, and most importantly, sincerity of welcome. For example, James visited a number of churches before deciding to be baptized in his local Roman Catholic Church. Many people with and without a learning disability like to attend the same church tradition as their family, but not always: Simon, for instance, preferred the lively music and worship of the Salvation Army to the more formal Anglican church of his parents. But in choosing a new church, an early step is to arrange a meeting between the disabled person and the priest or minister, who will have ideas how best to use the person's gifts in the church.

Before setting off for church

Help the person dress well and appropriately for church: we all love to look good! These days, it is less common to wear one's 'Sunday best'. However, it is true that dressing smartly on a Sunday can help many people with learning disabilities to feel the specialness of going to church, and projects a more positive image.

Ensure the person has a purse with money for the collection.

As far as possible help the person to be punctual: this allows them to choose a seat they like and to have the time necessary for transition and preparation for the service. It also means there is plenty of time to go to the toilet if necessary.

On arrival and before the service

If the person with a learning disability has a particular role or job at church, then support them to be ready for this, for example reminding the person when it is their turn on the rota for tea, for being a server, etc.

Make sure you know where the (disabled) toilets are!

In Roman Catholic churches, some may need support to dip their hand in the holy water and cross themselves.

In some churches, everyone puts on a name badge on arrival. If so, support the person to do this. In many churches, people greet each other as they arrive. Support the person to greet friends or to make new ones.

Most people have a favourite place to sit, near their friends.

Some churches project the hymns and songs on a screen, but many still use books or a service sheet: if so, find the right page and make sure the person is holding it the right way up. This may seem unnecessary for a person who cannot read, but as with so much else, it is about fitting in with the rest of the congregation.

Help the person prepare for the collection. It is worth noting that some people just want to get rid of all the coins in their purse, even if they cannot afford that amount, so don't be afraid to give discreet guidance. Doing this with the person before the service starts avoids fumbling in a purse when the plate comes round.

Lighting a candle in prayer before or after the service is a long tradition in some churches: for people who are non-verbal, such a participatory gesture can be especially meaningful. Some people can name a person they want to pray for, but for others, why not bring a small photo album to church? Then they can point to a photo of the person they want to pray for. For different reasons, not everyone finds holding the candle easy, and might appreciate you lighting it for them.

Some people with a disability also appreciate it if you take a minute to explain the flow of the service, and the theme of the readings. Full understanding is not the most important thing – what really matters is relationship, and the feeling of being included.

During the service

If a care worker is accompanying a person to church, the importance of showing respect cannot be overstated: for many, if not all, this shared meeting with God will be one of the most sacred moments in their week. Whether or not you are a believer yourself, or member of that church, your aim is to help the person you are accompanying to get as much as they can through full participation. For this reason, it is not acceptable to use one's mobile phone or read a novel or newspaper during the service! Your focus needs to be on the person you are accompanying. Each service is made up of different parts, with a variety of responses expected from the congregation. Some churches are livelier, others less so: in many, there are moments of stillness. But whatever the style, try and follow what you see others are doing. For instance, in Roman Catholic churches, members of the congregation bless themselves with the sign of the cross at the start and end of the service. Helping the person to respond appropriately sometimes means adapting to how the person is on the day, as much as to their general capacity. Sometimes a person just needs to sit down, even if everyone else is standing up or kneeling: use your common sense!

Giving a brief and discreet verbal explanation of a hymn or reading helps a person to follow more easily, as well as conveying your desire to be really attentive. For some, words don't work, but signing does, if you can do that. Others find it helpful just to follow key words such as 'Amen'. In Christine's church, every time her priest says 'Amen', Christine is renowned for adding her own loud and affirming 'A-MEN!' When she is absent, her voice is missed!

Supporting a person at communion time often requires particular thought: in many churches, this is the most sacred part of the service. What is the normal practice? Is it easier for the person to go up for communion, and if so when? Or is it easier for the priest or minister to come to where the person is sitting? If so, remember to sit somewhere convenient, and make sure the priest/minister remembers to come. Or, as happens in many Free churches, is communion passed down the pew, from member to member? This is useful to work out in advance if possible, with the priest or minister.

Another question concerns the actual taking of the communion elements as a particular person's practice might be to take only the bread, or only the wine, or just to dip the bread in the wine. Some people need support to only sip a little wine so there is enough for everyone else, while others need support to swallow the host or bread. Taking a drink of water at the same time works well for some but not all. If the communion elements are being passed down the pew, is it the custom to consume them immediately, or wait until everyone has been served? What to do if a person spits it out? Again, the advice is to discuss this whole area in advance with the priest or minister, aiming to help the person in their sacred moment of meeting with God.

At the end of the service

The weekly bulletin sheet does more than contain information about upcoming events: it is a sign of belonging. Ensure the person gets one to take home!

Many churches offer refreshments after the service: a good opportunity to greet old friends and make new ones. Many people, however, feel shy about how to communicate with a person who has few words, if any. For that reason, it can make all the difference when the support worker takes on the role of 'translator', helping each to understand what the other is saying. It could perhaps be the start of a new friendship.

On returning home

There are at least two ways that the bridging role continues on returning home: first, check the weekly church bulletin for upcoming events. These include coffee mornings, women's or men's group activities, special services, prayer meetings, house groups, church fêtes. If the person is willing and able to take part, then it is essential to mark the date and venue on the person's own calendar, so that their intention is seen by other relevant support people.

Second, help the person to share about their morning with others: what happened, old friends they chatted to, new friends they made, and of course the latest news.

Mid-week house groups, cell groups or services

In some churches, mid-week 'cell groups' play a key part in their tradition, where a few people regularly come together to deepen their faith by praying with the Gospel. How to help a person with learning disabilities participate? This is something to discuss with the priest or minister. Again, if this is done merely in a spirit of misguided charity, it will fail. The whole point is for the church to live out its own professed identity as the body of Christ, so that each person discovers and shares their gifts in service of his mission.

A church belonging form

This is for the person with a learning disability to fill in, with appropriate support from someone who knows them well. It could then go in the person's care plan. Photographs and drawings will both make it more 'user-friendly' and ensure the person themselves 'owns' it. (The form may be downloaded from the Canterbury Press website.)

CHURCH BELONGING

1 My church is called ....

....

Address ....

....

....

Telephone number ....

2 It is a .... church (religious tradition)

3 I have gone to this church since

....

4 The service I like to attend normally starts at ....

   and ends at ....

5 I am / am not baptized.

6 I am / am not confirmed.

7 I take / do not take communion.

   When taking communion I like to

   ....

   ....

   ....

   (e.g. only take the bread/dip the host in the wine).

   When taking communion I need/I do not need support.

8 The people I know at church are (include their birthday)

   ....

   ....

   ....

   ....

   ....

9 The priest / minister / leader is called ....

   ....

10 Another person at my church I can talk to for help and information is

   ....

   ....

   ....

   Telephone number ....

11   At church I like to do the following

(e.g. light a candle after the service, move around in my wheelchair)

....

....

....

12   When I am in church I normally sit (describe the place, and who I like to sit next to)

....

....

....

13   The things I don't like about church are

....

....

....

14   Areas I need support include the following (e.g. choosing a place to sit, not singing too loudly, finding the toilet, receiving Communion, communicating with people, arranging transport)

....

....

....

15   For the collection I normally give £

16   I regularly go to these events

....

....

....

PART 2

Towards creative inclusive church services

Ideas and suggestions for inclusive church services

To be read in conjunction with the section on specific ministries.

Worship is a sacred encounter with God, who desires to meet each person individually, in God's community, the church. Services aim to make this meeting a solemn but joyful and fruitful celebration in the life of each person, whatever their gifts and limitations, so that we can truly represent Christ to each other. Disability, of course, is no bar to this work of the Holy Spirit, who can use this reality to open our eyes to God's wider vision. Frances Young, a Methodist minister, once spent a week at the Othona Community with her son Arthur, who had a profound disability. Arthur loved the echoes in the church and would call out, just to hear the sound returning. One might imagine that this disturbed the prayerful atmosphere, but Frances Young remembers that one evening, 'Arthur suddenly seemed to be the Christ among us'.[3] It is not God that has a problem with a person's disability! All we need to do is risk another step into God's house of wider welcome. This means accepting the person with learning disabilities as they are, rather than always wanting them to conform to our expectations of normality. Jean Vanier speaks of 'the tyranny of normality'. So much depends on knowing the individual person, fine-tuning any support they need, in order that they can fully participate in the service, sharing their unique gifts as much as anyone else.

The following suggestions are ordered according to an Anglo-Catholic Eucharistic service, but the same elements will be found in most church services. A reminder: these are just starters – the aim is not to constrain your own imagination, but to stimulate it! Choose ideas that suit a particular service of whichever tradition and vary them. Enjoy being flexible and creative, keeping the needs of your church members in view. We are all on a learning curve.

Theme of the service

The first thing in planning a service is to decide the theme and the Bible readings. This might be decided by using the lectionary offered by your church. In this case the readings will be fixed and the theme must be chosen based on them. However, at times you may want to choose a theme for a special occasion and then you must choose readings which reflect the theme.

A general rule is that when we try to nourish people with learning disabilities, the whole congregation benefits. For instance, rather than just listening to a reading of the Gospel, it can be very powerful to see it being reverently mimed. Symbols can also speak volumes: after a reading of the story of the prodigal son, each member of the congregation was given a ring to keep as a reminder of the father's forgiveness. For a person without words, listening reflectively to music can be a profound experience: Franci, a young woman with profound disabilities in L'Arche in Chennai, would sit with tears streaming down her face, deeply touched when listening to classical music. On the other hand, Denis, a young man with Down's syndrome, becomes fully alive and dances with joy to upbeat praise songs!

How to decorate the church to bring out the theme? Rather than overdo the decor, it can be better to concentrate on one central focus. People with autism tend to get over-stimulated by too many symbols, sounds and smells. Simplicity brings clarity! For instance, at a service to welcome a new church member, paper fishes and nets were placed in front of the altar, to recall the calling of the first disciples, along with the 'Ichthus' fish symbol to represent Jesus. At another church, the New Year service began with each member of the congregation entering via an arch of ribbons and coloured cloths, symbolizing the movement from the old year to the new. For a service on refugees, the central focus could be a flimsy raft recalling the desperate risks taken by all those attempting to sail to Europe.

Consider changing the way the chairs are placed: formal rows, horseshoe, or circle, as befits a particular style of service or a particular liturgical season.

THE ORDER OF SERVICE

Gathering

Ways of welcoming to build the sense of community:

- Give each person something appropriate as people enter the church, e.g. a candle, a card to be filled out or coloured in …
- Invite people to spend a couple of minutes speaking to their neighbour.
- Try signing the initial greeting. A person with a learning disability could assist in this sometimes.

Penitential rite/Confession

- It is important to convey to everyone, not least to people with learning disabilities, that they are loved just as they are today.
- Repetition helps, e.g. sung responses.

- Use simple words.
- Invite people to think about one or two times in the past week where they have been angry, or not loving – and then say sorry by asking God to give us mercy, for instance by simply singing 'Lord have mercy'.

The Word

- Read the Gospel as a guided imaginative contemplation, inviting people into the scene with questions for reflection and allowing some moments of silence for this.
- Mime the Gospel. The action can be frozen at various points so people can reflect on what is going on, e.g. in a L'Arche mime of the parable of the banquet, the people watching were invited to look at the face of God to see his reaction to the rich refusing his invitation to the feast. They were asked to say in a few words how they felt seeing the sadness on God's face. (See below for suggestions on how to do this: pp. 28–32).
- People could write or draw their personal response to the reading on slips of paper which could be given at the offertory.
- Simplify the reading to its essence.
- Tell the story rather than read it. (See below for suggestions on how to do this: p. 26).
- Use visual aids.
- Invite people to engage with the reading by sharing their response with a neighbour.

Prayers of Intercession

- Invite a person with a learning disability to read out a prayer.
- Give space for anyone, including people with learning disabilities, to pray spontaneously from where they are sitting.
- Have a time of silence where people could write or draw on a suitably shaped piece of card, e.g. an apple shape (giving thanks for fruits), or a dove (for peace), or tears (for people who grieve). These could be collected and taken up in a basket at the offertory.
- Use a symbolic action, e.g. each person could come forward and light a candle.

The Offertory

This is the time when we offer our humanity to God, our daily life, work, home and leisure. Bread and wine, as well as the collection plates, are often included in an offertory procession, as well as what the children's liturgy group or Sunday school have been making. But other symbolic objects could also be offered in line with the theme, e.g. a loaf of bread, two fish; a fishing net; a cross; hearts; water ...
Other suggestions:

- A gesture (for instance, standing up or raising arms) as a sign that we offer ourselves.
- Have a procession with music and dancing.
- A person in a wheelchair could take up the offering.

Exchange of Peace

This is the time when we show that we are a community of Jesus' friends.
Some suggestions:

- Turn to the immediate neighbours in front and behind as well as the people on either side who may be friends or family already. Speak to them. Ask their name.
- Servers (who could include a person with a learning disability) offer peace at the end of each row and then the peace is passed along the row.
- Invite people to do the gesture of 'Namaste' (hands folded together as in prayer) explaining the Indian symbolism: God present in my heart honours God present in your heart.
- Use the Makaton sign or another sign language for peace.
- Sing a peace song with actions that you can invent, e.g. 'Peace before us' by David Haas; or 'You are the face of God' by Karen Drucker.
- In smaller groups it is possible to share the peace around the altar: the priest or minister begins, and the 'peace' travels round the circle, one by one till it comes back to the first person. This shows that the peace ultimately comes through Christ who is the one who reconciles us.

The Eucharist/Holy Communion

Some suggestions:

- For the Lord's Prayer: sign it; sing it; encourage people to say it in their own language; hold hands for the prayer so all are united.
- Invite everyone to mirror some of the gestures made by the priest.

- Sometimes vary the wording of the consecration of the Holy Communion elements, to include people with disabilities explicitly – an adapted prayer is included in this book (see pp. 32–3).
- All stand in a circle round the altar/communion table.
- Give communion FIRST to those who cannot come forward so they do not have to wait and be the last to receive.
- Have a silent Eucharist or Holy Communion. Lots of ideas for such a service can be found online.
- Invite people to name out loud, or to hold up photos of those who have died, or who are sick. The photos are a way of including people who cannot speak with words.
- Send people in pairs, including a person with a learning disability, to take Holy Communion to the housebound.

Church notices

These are about the ongoing life of the church community during the week.

- The invitation to coffee afterwards could be said by a person with a learning disability.
- Invite people to share news.
- Sing 'Happy Birthday' to those who are celebrating a special birthday. The Stevie Wonder version makes a cheerful alternative to the well-known tune, and can be found on YouTube. You can add verses such as 'May God bless you'.

The Sending

This is when we are sent out again into the world, to take Christ's message of love to all those we meet during the coming week.

- Repeat the main message in one line as something to take away and reflect on.
- Give people something that links with the theme as a reminder to take home, e.g.
  - a bookmark with an appropriate prayer or quote and an image, e.g. for Lent or for Advent.
  - a symbol that recalls the theme, e.g. a dove-shaped piece of paper, a leaf, a seed, an apple, salt, Easter eggs, sweets, a footprint …
  - Blessed bread to share with people at home.
  - A different symbol each week of a particular season such as Advent or Lent, e.g. for the Sundays over the Easter season: a small cut-out card fish (the risen Jesus by the lake), a flower (Mary Magdalen meeting Jesus in the garden), bread (on the road to Emmaus) …

- A prayer bag for a particular season: this could include a page of instructions on how to use the bag using paper the colour of the liturgical season, symbols for the seasons, reflections on the symbols, prayer cards. Be creative! Ideas can be found online, e.g. www.buildfaith.org/lent-in-a-bag
- Challenge people to take risks in sharing the gospel with someone familiar or with someone new, e.g. a neighbour, elderly people, the homeless ...
- Sprinkle water over the people as a sending blessing.
- Invite people to turn and face the open door as we are sent out into the world. The priest/minister then gives the blessing facing the congregation from the back.

Eight basic guidelines

1 An adult with learning disabilities is just as much an adult as anyone else: but this does not preclude activities that bring out the childlike qualities which Jesus asks us all to develop.
2 One strong symbol is usually enough! Too many can be confusing, and some people can quickly get sensory overload.
3 Introduce the theme and symbol at the start of the service and refer to it throughout.
4 Simple, clear, concrete words, in short sentences.
5 Allow spontaneity – don't overcontrol. This allows people to take the initiative.
6 Trust the Holy Spirit to speak through your own inner creativity and wisdom.
7 Evaluate what works.
8 Enjoy!

Opening up Scripture with people with learning disabilities

You will have your own experience on making the material accessible but here are some possible ideas you may find helpful:

Choosing a Bible passage

A story about people can work better than something abstract and intellectual. Passages that have concrete symbols such as light, salt, bread work well. For inspiration about how to choose:

JESUS AND FRIENDS,

- Try the Gospel reading for the day (the Roman Catholic and Anglican churches have lectionaries that can be consulted).
- Think about the time of year, the season, what is going on in the world, what is happening for the group of people or individuals within it.

Preparation for reading/telling the story: S – E – T – S!

Adapt the reading so people with learning disabilities can understand it:

- S – Keep it Short.
- E – Identify the Essence of the story and find a way to communicate this clearly.
- T – Check different Translations of the Bible: the book list in the Appendixes has suggestions. Books such as *I Meet Jesus* by Jean Vanier have lots of simple clear line drawings that are not childish. This book could be used in small groups by showing the pictures, or in church by just reading the shortened, simplified texts.
- S – Simplify difficult words and concepts – refer to the Glossary of 'Church-speak' in the Appendixes for ideas of how to do this.

Guidelines in preparing a Bible passage for people with learning disabilities to read

- Keep sentences short – they should be no more than 10 to 15 words.
- Each sentence should have just one idea and one verb.
- Make sentences active not passive: 'Jesus healed the girl' (active) not 'The girl was healed by Jesus' (passive).
- Take out words that are not needed, for example, say 'for 14 days' not 'for a period of 14 days'; 'two weeks' is even better.
- If you need to use difficult words or ideas, say what they mean – do this in the next sentence, not as part of the same sentence.
- Give the context which may mean summarizing the story before the actual reading starts.

Supporting a person with learning disabilities to read the Bible passage: P – R – i –S – M – S

It can be a real gift when a person with a learning disability, who is able, reads the passage for the group. Their reading of the passage can at times enable listeners to hear the story in a new way. For example, Ruby reads exceedingly slowly but very clearly. Listening to her read can be a powerful experience, the audience hanging on every word.

Here are some tips:

- P – When Printing the reading for a reader with learning disabilities use:
  - 14-point font size aligned to the left and with plenty of white space
  - a sans-serif or Arial typeface
  - matt paper stock to prevent glare.
- R – Rehearsing beforehand can iron out some difficulties, helping to overcome any lack of confidence with difficult words.
- S – Support: Confidence can be given when a person stands at the side of someone with a learning disability who can read. The support person can prompt with the very occasional difficult word if absolutely necessary. (If the person needs a lot of prompts then it is not fair to ask them to read publicly and so embarrass them.)
- M – A Microphone helps and gives confidence to those who can read well but have very soft voices.
- S – Encourage them to read Slowly and clearly.

When a person can read but is difficult to understand, then the passage could be re-read by someone else afterwards: not as a 'better' way to read, but in order to allow the words to go deeper. This must be done respectfully and not as if just correcting the first reading.

After reading a simplified version, the full Bible passage could then be read for those able to understand in a more cerebral way. Those who understand at a heart and body level will follow the full passage more easily after hearing a more accessible version.

The importance of telling the story – rather than reading it

It can help people with learning disabilities if the reading is *told as a story*, directly to the listeners, rather than read. Looking at the listeners rather than at the page of a book is much more likely to keep their attention, and means that the teller can respond more straightforwardly to their reactions. The teller must know the story well and have confidence to tell rather than read.

Including the listeners

Think creatively and imaginatively as you prepare how to tell the story. Here are some ideas on how to include the listeners (only do what is comfortable for you!). You could, for instance, invite the listeners to join in with actions, e.g. holding their arms up like the branches of a tree, or moving their hands to give the sense of rain falling. You do the actions yourself and encourage people to mirror you. You can encourage listeners to make sounds appropriate to the story, e.g. birds singing, the wind or rain.

Some examples

The story of Noah

Narrator   Clouds began to cover the sky. Can you all do as I am doing?

Rub the palms of your hands together.

The rain began to fall, slowly at first.

Begin to click your fingers, slowly then faster as everyone joins in.

Then the rain fell more heavily.

Start clapping your hands.

Then there was a real thunderstorm.

Slap your thighs with your hands and stamp your feet. As the narrator, use your voice to give the mood: gentle for the light rain, louder for the thunderstorm. For silence, suddenly spread your arms wide as if cutting off the sound, and/or put a finger to your lips.

The story of Jesus calming the sea

Narrator   Suddenly there was a great wind.

Make the sound of wind and throw your arms as if making a wind and encourage everyone to copy you.

The story of creation

Narrator   Then God made the birds ...

Begin to whistle, then cup your hands as if listening, encouraging everyone to make the sounds of birds.

Images, props, photos, percussion instruments can be very useful. Godly Play props can be very helpful in small groups (see the Appendix for the website). For the sound of water, rain-sticks can be used; for the sound of the sea an ocean drum can be used (a drum that creates sounds like gentle or crashing waves).

Alternatively, why not act out the passage, or find an appropriate action that involves each person. In the samples of church services below, you will find suggestions for acting out Bible stories.

Imaginative Contemplation can be effective with people with learning disabilities. It is a powerful way to help people to enter into the story themselves. First, tell the Bible story. Then tell it again slowly and invite people to imagine what they see, hear, touch, smell, taste. Take time over this. Ask questions to help them.

Lectio Divina can also be very fruitful. For this, tell the story slowly and clearly using simple words. Then ask if there was one word or image that they remember. Repeat this word, or image. Invite the person to remember it as something important that God wants to say to them today.

In certain situations, one might consider *Audio Divina* (simply sitting listening to music in a prayerful way), *Visio Divina* (spending time looking at a striking image), or *Natura Divina* (sitting in nature quietly and looking at a tree, some clouds or a flower, being truly present in the moment). Each offers a way of 'stilling', becoming aware of God who is present, listening and encouraging.

Jean Vanier's words well express the essence of the issue:

> The logic and content of what is said is less important than the faith and love with which it is conveyed. The tone of voice shows whether the speaker wants to seem brilliant and knowledgeable, or whether he wants to nourish, to give freely and witness humbly to what has been given and freely received. The talks which nourish come from people who allow God to speak through their lips.[4]

In other words, heart speaks to heart. James Finley, a contemplative, says that words can wash over us and not be understood, but that which comes from the deepest depths of us speaks to the deepest depths of the listener.

How to prepare inclusive mimes
on Scripture stories

Mimes can be a very effective way to help people with learning disabilities to use their gifts in church services or small group celebrations, bringing fresh understanding of a Bible passage to each person. Instead of the congregation just listening to the reading, mimes give another route to engage with the passage visually. This helps people to enter more fully into the story rather than just listening to it being read. Repeating the same drama year after year can help people to become very familiar with it. In many L'Arche communities, some stations of the cross are acted out on Good Friday, followed on Easter Sunday by a mime of the appearance of Jesus to Mary Magdalen in the garden. As the years go by, the story becomes more and more known at a deeper level.

People with learning disabilities are often very spontaneous, and their way of reacting in a mime to the story can reveal new insights. In one mime of the prodigal son, the person playing the prodigal son could not bear the older brother not being part of the final celebration. He went over to the older brother and *insisted* on him joining in the celebrating.

For those watching such a re-enactment, there can be unexpected discoveries too. Hazel remembers that after a L'Arche group had acted out the story of creation at Greenbelt, a Christian festival in the UK, an Anglican priest came over to say that her whole theology had been turned upside down by the mime: 'A person with a learning disability playing the part of God? This was a new way of understanding God.' But that was not all: what really hit home were the words, 'in his own image, he created them'. For the actors had been chosen for their ability to act the different roles, irrespective of any disability or not: this meant that a 'disabled' God created Adam, who was also played by a man with a disability; and Eve, who had no visible disabilities. It was the combination of word and action that made the priest rethink her image of God and what it means to be created in God's image. And such experiences are not uncommon.

Below are some suggestions for creating a mime based on a Bible story. Golden rules include:

- Feel free to use your own creativity.
- Enjoy bringing a Bible story to life.
- Be open to the new insights that may be revealed.
- Go with the flow and accept the unexpected and unplanned!

But first, a caveat: just as much as anyone else, people with learning disabilities can love being centre-stage – who does not love the limelight and applause? But the aim must be to draw out the person's real acting skill, so that they really enter into their character, and bring depth to their part. This means, clearly, going deeper than just acting for laughs, and encouraging them to act from a deeper, truer, more grounded place in themselves. Their performances then can be very powerful. Indeed, some can enter so fully into their roles it is important to 'de-role' them well at the end, to avoid, for instance, the actor who plays 'God' staying in role for hours after!

What touches an audience is when actors are fully in their role, and not showing off themselves. When watching a performance of the story of Moses and the burning bush, the audience needs to be able to see Moses, and not 'Johnnie' being himself but in the costume of Moses, and adding in funny asides to get attention by making people laugh.

- Create a script based on the Bible reading you have chosen but using simple words. Cut out what is not essential. When narrating keep to the script as repetition helps people with learning disabilities to remember what they are supposed to do. But also feel free to improvise when it is necessary and appropriate.
- There are several ways you can work with the script:
  - Telling and acting the story straight through.
  - Stopping the action at crucial points, then giving questions for reflection and allowing time for people to respond.
  - Having one or two narrators telling the story and reading the dialogue, the actors miming what they hear. These narrators can interact playfully with each other.

- Allowing space for the main characters to repeat key words, or to say a line on their own if they can. In this case give a clear prompt with key words or phrases, e.g. Narrator: Then Jesus said, 'Mary!' ...
  The person playing Jesus repeats: Mary!
  OR the narrator simply waits after saying 'Then Jesus said ...' for the actor to say 'Mary'. This needs rehearsal!
- Allowing the actors to speak their lines on their own while the narrator sticks with the narration. This can only be done with the most capable of actors. Many people with learning disabilities would have trouble learning lines, or speaking clearly and projecting enough to be heard.

• Rehearse with the same person each time as the narrator then the actors become used to the cues they need.

• It can be absolutely fine to include comedy, as well as to go with the flow when a person with learning disabilities spontaneously comes up with a good phrase. For instance, Donna, acting as the woman who had lost one of her coins, told the audience who were all standing up and searching for the lost coin to 'Work harder!' She was very insistent and kept repeating 'Work harder!' They did! And the coin was found! This led to everyone doing a simple circle dance in celebration, then ended with space for serious reflection. What can touch people profoundly is this balance of moods and tempo: comedy leading to silence and serious reflection, drama leading to prayer, action leading to stillness.

• The way you narrate will help cue the actors. For example, 'Peter and John ran back to the upper room.' You notice the actors are going the wrong way! and say, 'Peter and John ran back to the upper room – which was on the other side!' as you emphasize the words and point in the right direction.

Or in another case: 'Jesus went up the mountain to pray and then in the morning he returned to his friends.' (You notice Jesus is staying too long up the mountain.) 'Jesus stayed for *many* hours praying to his father! Then he (said with great emphasis!) *returned* to his friends!' If this still does not work, walk over to 'Jesus' and gently guide him to the right place as you continue to narrate. Paradoxically, if you do this in an obvious way, it is less obtrusive and more reassuring to the onlookers than otherwise.

An audience can feel uncomfortable for the actors if things go 'wrong' and you try to cover up the mistake. However, they can relax, and even enjoy it, when the mistake is made obvious in a way that is respectful and neither shaming or mocking. It has been known, in a mime of the Noah story, for the PowerPoint showing the 40 days of falling rain to start too early ... so the narrator improvised, 'Ah, here you see Noah's dream of what the rain would be like. The actual rain will fall a bit later when God gives the command!'

• Go with the flow and improvise. Hazel remembers the same drama of Noah's ark: the 'raven' flew away up one side aisle. The 'dove' then flew up the other aisle. The 'raven' got confused so turned back and flew after the 'dove'. At this point, Hazel needed to improvise spontaneously: 'The dove flew away – er … followed by its shadow!' This means you name the mistake and allow it, and then carry on, rather than desperately trying to hide the fact that something has gone wrong! The audience then laugh with you rather than feeling uncomfortable for the people onstage.

- Ensure there are support people. In a nativity play, if 'Joseph' is a person with learning disabilities, then it can help that 'Mary' is not, so she can guide him if necessary, or vice versa. Or, there could be a 'servant' to give any necessary support. There could also be people at the sides to give the cue as to when an actor should enter or come off stage.
- It is good for people with and without learning disabilities to act together.
- Many people with learning disabilities respond better to personal names for God rather than abstract ones such as 'Lord'. Therefore, where possible in the script use words such as 'Jesus', or 'God our Father'.
- Large visible props are needed. If light is a key symbol to be used in a church service, a small night-light would be completely lost compared to a tall candle. A well-known mantra from drama college is: make it bigger!
- Any gestures need to be large, direct and clear. For example, if you want to point to someone, then your intention will be much more obvious if your arm is stretched out straight and confidently in the right direction, than if it is bent with your elbow tucked into the body.
- Be aware of sight lines. The audience wants to see faces not bums! It can help in rehearsals to demonstrate yourself with the actors watching, i.e. ask the actors to sit where the audience will sit. Then stand talking to someone in the acting area, first with your back to the audience, then at an angle so your face can be seen. Ask them which position works best.
- Facial expressions are very important. It can help just to rehearse clear facial expressions: sad, happy, fearful, prayerful …
- Rainbow cloths are a great asset being so versatile: we recommend buying seven two-metre cloths made of butter muslin, each one of the colours of the rainbow. They can be bought in any Indian fabric store. Bright colours rather than pastel colours are better as they stand out more sharply. These can be supplemented with cloths of white, black and brown. They all need to be kept clean and well folded or ironed so they do not look crumpled and last longer. These cloths can be used in many varied ways:
  - As simple stoles to distinguish different roles, e.g. white for God or for Jesus; other colours for the disciples; purple for Pilate.
  - To decorate a prayer space.
  - To use as headbands or belts, e.g. for the pirates who captured St Patrick when he was young.
  - To create landscapes: green and brown for the earth; yellow for the sun; blue for springs of living water, a river, a lake, a rainbow …

- To cover furniture or parts of the space so that people are not distracted.
- If props are put on a table, then a cloth can beautify the table.
- If the actors are in black clothes, this can be especially effective: long-sleeved tops, vest (so no flesh shows when arms are lifted), trousers, socks and shoes (unless people are barefoot. Black is a neutral colour. The coloured cloths can be simple additions to create characters, along with the use of props.
- Rehearse so that people understand the importance of staying in the role from the moment they begin to come onstage until they are offstage.
- Work on helping people to stay in a 'frozen' position in their role. Such postures can be very effective, as you will see in some of the sample services: in 'freezing', the actors become like living icons for the audience to contemplate.
- Ensure there are chairs available for anyone unable to stand for a long time; similarly, some people will need help to go up or down any stairs leading to the stage area.
- The actors could easily include a person in a wheelchair, or with visual impairment. For instance, Susan cannot see, but with the support of a friend, she makes an excellent star in the nativity play. Another example is Michael, who uses a wheelchair: he makes an excellent Herod or Pilate as these characters do not necessarily have to move around much. The person who pushes his wheelchair can be the king's servant. But he can also be a good donkey, if called upon, Mary putting her bags on his front tray and Joseph pushing his wheelchair.
- Try to avoid the situation where a person with learning disabilities with an important role needs to be pushed around by a non-actor in order to get to where they need to be. It is much less intrusive to have someone in a role, giving support: e.g. the 'Archangel Gabriel' can have some 'support' angels. And it is quite fitting for 'Herod' to have a courtier by his side discreetly guiding him to look or face the right way.

Exploring ways of dramatizing Bible stories as part of a group of people with and without learning disabilities can be fun, moving, inspiring and very rewarding. The purpose is always for each person to enter more deeply into these stories and find fresh insights. The drama becomes a form of praying, connecting with God. Such a group, when they really work as a team together without showing off, can move an audience: to tears, to laughter, to deep stillness, then to an awareness of God who is present with them.

An adapted Holy Communion Prayer

Prepared by Revd Peter Cole, a Methodist Minister who has a physical disability, for the ecumenical Sarum Impairment and Spirituality weekend conference 2008 for persons who have serious disabling conditions and for carers.

God of mystery,
Known through the crucified,
Whose power refashions weakness and strength,
Whose presence is embodied through brokenness,
We offer our awe and wonder.

With those who are broken by pain,
With those exhausted by the struggle to conform,
With those crippled by the insensitivity of others,
With those not seen as a resource but only as a concern,
We praise you saying,

Holy, holy, holy
God of vulnerable love,
Heaven and Earth proclaim your glory,
Hosanna in the highest,
Blessed is he who reveals
The reality of God.

We bless the name of Jesus,
Bone of our bone,
Flesh of our flesh,
Whose brokenness and suffering make love real,
Who on the night in which he was betrayed
Took bread, gave thanks, broke it and gave it to his disciples saying,
'Take, eat. This is my body which is for you.
Do this in remembrance of me.'
After supper he took the cup saying,
'Drink from this, all of you, this is my blood given for you.
Do this whenever you drink it in remembrance of me!

Christ has died,
Christ has risen,
Christ redeems our stories.

Therefore as we eat this bread and drink this cup
We acknowledge brokenness as a path to truth.
We long for the bread of tomorrow:
Eternally broken and so able to nourish.
We long for the new wine of the kingdom:
Continuously poured out that thirst may be quenched.

Spirit of wisdom, brood over these bodily things
And make us one body with Christ
So that in the life of a changing church:
The broken may lead us towards wholeness,
The suffering show us the way to peace
And the excluded teach us of community,
So that all may receive
The gifts to be found
Within the body of Christ.

PART 3

Twelve examples of services

Introduction

These 12 examples are designed for trying out in church services. They each include a fairly simple mime. In preparing the service, it will be helpful to read each in link with the section in Part 1, 'How to prepare inclusive mimes on Scripture stories'. The title 'narrator' is used in some places, rather than the title 'reader': this is to show that the task involved is often not simply reading the text, but amplifying it, through repetition, or question, etc.

1 The call of Abraham

This service could be used when a person with a learning disability leaves their childhood home for their own home, when a parishioner or priest leaves, when refugees are welcomed, when there is a new beginning for people or for the parish, for students going to university, when the reading occurs in the lectionary ...

Possible themes

Call – blessing – trust – new beginnings – leaving the old for the new.

You will need

Actors

- God – a white robe or shawl, or a priest's white alb.
- Abraham – a staff, with a brown cloak.
- Sarah – a shawl.
- Lot – a bag or a cloth filled with oddments and tied up in a bundle to carry.
- Terah, Abraham's father – an old man's shawl, headdress.

Props

- Stones to make an altar.
- Baskets.
- Coloured pens.

Preparation

- Rehearse the narrator and the scenes with the living icons.
- Be clear about where Abraham will travel and where he will stop.
- Teach people the 'Bush Beatitudes' song by John Coleman (see Songs Appendix).
- Ensure there is someone to read the intercessions.
- Prepare little cards with the image of Abraham in the desert setting out on his journey – enough for one per person *(see p. 37)*.

Decoration

Project the image of Abraham in the desert setting out on his journey in the church, or place it at the entrance of the church so that each person can see it as they come in.

THE WORD Genesis 12.1–9

Read the whole story from the Bible first for those who can understand, or read this simplified version:

Narrator There was once a man called Abram, later known as Abraham. God said to him, 'Go, leave your home and country and go to a new country which I will show you. I promise to bless you and your children.'
Abraham did as God told him. He, his wife Sarah and his nephew Lot left their home and country and went to a new country. Then God spoke to him again, 'I will give this land to you and your children.' Abraham built an altar there where he prayed to God.

Repeat the story and create living icons with chosen actors:

Narrator God told Abraham, 'Go, leave your home and country. I promise to bless you and your children.'

Abraham and God go and stand in front of the congregation, facing each other but so their faces can both be seen. Or God faces the congregation and Abraham stands facing God with his back to the congregation. They then freeze. Abraham is standing looking up as if listening to the voice of God; if possible, God is standing high up in front of him, looking down at him. Sarah, Lot and Terah stand at the side watching.

The celebrant offers a reflection on the scene about the importance of listening to God and finishes with a question:

Celebrant   Where do I hear the voice of God in my life today? Take some time in silence now to reflect on this.

Allow some time of silence.

Celebrant   Now share any thoughts that came to you with a neighbour.

Allow time for this.

SONG   'Bush Beatitudes' by John Coleman, first verse and chorus (see Songs Appendix).

Narrator   Abraham did as God told him. He, his wife Sarah and his nephew Lot, left their home and country and went to a new country.

Abraham holding his staff and with his arm around Sarah, Lot carrying a bag, begin to walk away from Abraham's father who stands looking sad. They freeze: Abraham, Sarah and Lot facing away from the father, but looking back at him. The father stands still with a hand raised in blessing.

The celebrant offers a reflection on the scene on the theme of following God's call into the unknown and finishes with a question:

Celebrant   When have I left a familiar life and taken a step in trust into the unknown? Take some time in silence now to reflect on this.

Allow some time for this.

Celebrant   Now share any thoughts that came to you with a neighbour.

Allow some time for this.

SONG   'Bush Beatitudes', second verse and chorus.

Narrator   Then God spoke to Abraham again, 'I will give this land to you and your children.'

Abraham, Sarah and Lot walk further along the road. God appears to them and blesses them. They freeze, Abraham, Sarah and Lot with hands folded in prayer and looking down reverently. God with both hands raised in blessing over them.

The celebrant offers a reflection on the scene on the theme of the confirmation of an original step of faith and the appearance of God in our lives, and finishes with a question:

Celebrant   When have I experienced an affirmation of a choice I have made? Take some time in silence now to reflect on this.

Allow some time of silence.

Celebrant   Now share any thoughts that came to you with a neighbour.

Allow some time for this.

SONG   *'Bush Beatitudes', third verse and chorus.*

Narrator   Abraham built an altar there where he prayed to God.

Abraham makes an altar of some stones and then kneels, hands folded in prayer, to pray before the altar, looking up to heaven.

The celebrant offers a reflection on the scene on the theme of the importance of worshipping God, praying to him and giving thanks, and finishes with a question:

Celebrant   Do I take time to stop, notice and give thanks? Take some time in silence now to reflect on this.

Allow some time of silence.

Celebrant   Now share any thoughts that came to you with a neighbour.

Allow time for this.

SONG   *'Bush Beatitudes', fourth verse and chorus.*

PRAYERS OF INTERCESSION

(Reword these as you wish using simple words and short phrases.)

Celebrant   We pray for people who are forced to leave home, e.g. refugees, exiles.
We pray for people who are looking for God's call in their life.
We pray that we might trust God in our lives.
We pray for those people who are examples of trust and courage.
We pray for the Jewish, Christian and Muslim descendants of Abraham, that they might live in harmony and strive for peace.

OFFERTORY

A procession with:

- Bread.
- Wine.
- Abraham's staff symbolizing going on a journey in faith.
- The bag carried by Lot symbolizing the offering of our humanity, just as we are.

Lay the staff and bag at the altar or communion table in thanksgiving.

SENDING

Give out small copies of image of Abraham in the desert setting out on his journey to each person where they are sitting. The cards could be in baskets along with some coloured pens which could be handed out as well.

Celebrant   I invite you now to take a few moments to think of what steps you want to commit yourself to on the journey of this coming week. Draw or write on the back of the card, or colour the picture in.

Now take these cards home as a reminder of Abraham stepping out in faith on a journey that changed his life, and of what you commit yourselves to this week.

2   The call of Moses

This service could be used when the church is making a commitment to others in need e.g. welcoming a refugee family or opening doors to the homeless, or for someone becoming a missionary, or when the reading occurs in the lectionary.

Possible themes

The call of God – God's preferential love for the vulnerable, marginalized people – recognizing God in the ordinariness of daily life – lives being transformed – making a commitment in the light of faith.

You will need

Actors

A narrator.
God – a white robe.
Moses – a staff, a brown cloak, shoes or sandals.

Props

- A burning bush – a hanging of a collage of a burning bush, maybe made by the Sunday school/children's liturgy group, or several lit candles, or a projection of an image of a fire, or flame-coloured cloths with logs positioned to look like a fire.

Preparation

- A notice at the entrance inviting everyone to remove their shoes in the hallway, porch or narthex before entering the main body of the church. Or a pair of people could invite them to do this. Shoes could be left there until people leave at the end.
- Or instead, invite people to take off their shoes before going up for communion.
- Rehearse the meeting of God and Moses.
- Have slips of paper and pencils or pens for the people in each row of seats.

Decoration

- Project the icon of Moses and the Burning Bush in the church, or display it at the entrance so people see it as they come in (see p. 42).

THE WORD Exodus 3.1–15

Read the whole story from the Bible first for those who can understand, or read a simplified version:

Narrator	Long before Jesus was born, there was a man called Moses. He was living in the desert looking after sheep. One day he came to a mountain where he saw a bush that was burning and heard the voice of God coming from the bush. God called to him, 'Moses, Moses!' Moses replied, 'Here I am.' God told him, 'Don't come any closer. Take off your sandals for you are standing on holy ground. I am the God of your fathers.'
	Moses was afraid to look at God.
	God said, 'I have seen the suffering of my people in the land of Egypt. I will save them and lead them to a land that is good. I am going to send you to the king of Egypt, the Pharaoh.'
	Moses replied, 'Who am I to go to the Pharaoh or to lead your people out of Egypt?' God replied, 'I will be with you.'
	Moses said, 'When people ask me who sent me, what shall I say?'

God said, 'Tell them, my name is I am who I am. It is I who has sent you to them.'
Moses listened to God.

Have three readers: Narrator, Moses, God; during the narration, the actor playing Moses approaches the altar, removes his shoes and listens and responds to God's voice.

Repeat the story with God and Moses acting out the meeting as indicated below.

There are different ways of doing this: God and Moses could say their lines, or the narrator could say the lines for them, in which case the narrator needs to say each time, 'God said ...' etc.

Narrator   Moses was looking after his sheep in the desert. Then he saw in front of him a bush that was burning. He heard the voice of God calling him.

Moses walks up the central aisle towards the 'fire'. When he notices it, he stops, looks in astonishment and listens.

God   Moses, Moses.

God appears behind the bush and looks at Moses.

Moses   Here I am, Lord.

Moses bows before God and opens his arms wide.

God   Take off your shoes for you are standing on holy ground. I am the God of your fathers, the God of Abraham.

Moses takes off his sandals.

SONG   *'This is holy ground, we're standing on holy ground' by Christopher Beatty.*

Narrator   Moses was afraid to look at God.

Moses looks down and covers his face with his hands.

God   I have seen how sad my people are and how much they suffer as slaves in Egypt. I will save them and lead them to a good land of milk and honey. I want you to go to the king of Egypt to tell him to let my people go.

God points as if to Egypt.

Moses   Who am I to do that? I can't do that!

Moses looks up, shrugging his shoulders.

God   I will be with you.

God holds out his hands to Moses.

Moses   Who shall I say sent me? What is your name? Who are you?

Moses lifts his shoulders and arms in a questioning gesture.

God   Tell them, my name is: I am who I am. I am the one who sends you.

God spreads his arms wide.

Narrator   Moses listened to God.

Moses bows to God.

SONG   *'Here I am, Lord, is it I, Lord?' by Daniel L. Schutte.*

Actors go off at the end of the song.

The celebrant offers a reflection based on the following questions:

Celebrant   Do I hear God calling me by name in my life?
Do I recognize holy ground in my daily life?
Can I reply 'Here I am' to a call of God to help others? Even when it means doing something I am afraid of or feel incapable of? Whose cries am I hearing? Who is crying today? Who is bringing out compassion in me? What is the call for me today? Can I trust God's promise to be with me today? I invite you now to take a few moments to reflect on these questions, then write down or draw on the slips of paper you found on your seats: whose cry for help do I hear in my life today? In what way do I feel unable to respond? How can I trust that God is with us?

Alternatively this could be a time of sharing with a neighbour.

Allow time for this.

Another song that could be used is 'Moses, take your shoes off, you're on holy ground' by Jessy Dixon (very lively; to be found on YouTube).

PRAYERS OF INTERCESSION

(Reword as you wish using simple words and short phrases.)

Celebrant   We pray for people who feel they are no good, who lack confidence.
We pray that we might trust our gifts and risk using them.
We pray for national leaders to guide their people wisely.
We pray for today's hidden slaves.
We pray for courage to challenge injustice and to respond to the calls we hear.

OFFERTORY/COLLECTION

Celebrant   I invite you to put in the collection plate the slip of paper you wrote or drew on earlier. These symbolize how we offer our lives, just as we are, with all our fears and feelings of not being good enough, trusting that God is calling us and will be with us.

Along with the bread and wine, take up a large flame-coloured candle as a reminder of the burning bush, and of God's presence.

SENDING

Give each person a small card of the icon of Moses and the Burning Bush as a reminder of God's call in our lives with the words, 'Here I am' on the back and the Bible reference, Exodus 3.4.

Celebrant   I invite you to take these cards home as a reminder of the name of God: *I am who I am*. Our God is a God of the present moment. Here and now he is with us, and he calls us as he called Moses to help his people, to lead them out of misery.
Think too of Moses' words to God, 'Here I am.' Can we too say that?
This week may you listen out for God's call in your life to help others, and be ready to respond to God, 'Here I am.'

3   The call of Mary

This could be used in Advent, or for new beginnings.

Possible themes

Listening to God – being willing to say yes to God – meeting God in daily life.

Preparation

- Make enough A8 cards for one per person of the photo of the statuette of Mary on one side, and on the other, the quotation 'Let it be done in me according to your word'.
- Place the cards with the image of Mary on each seat before people enter.
- Ask a few people to be prepared to say a prayer out loud during the intercessions and to respond 'Amen' to the prayer of anyone else.

Decoration

Project an image of the annunciation in the church (you can google 'images of the annunciation' then choose one you like), or display it at the entrance so people see it as they come in.

THE WORD Luke 1.26–38

Read the whole story from the Bible first, or read the simplified version below:

Narrator	The angel Gabriel was sent by God to a young woman who lived in the town of Nazareth. Her name was Mary. She was going to marry Joseph. The angel said to her, 'Rejoice Mary. Be happy. God is really pleased with you. He is with you.' Mary was confused by his words. Gabriel said, 'Don't be afraid Mary. God is really pleased with you. You are going to have a baby boy. You will call him Jesus. He will be the Son of God and will be the king of God's people.' Mary didn't understand and asked how all this would happen. Gabriel said, 'This will happen through the Holy Spirit and the power of God. So you can believe my words, I tell you that your elderly cousin, Elizabeth, who is too old to have children, is also expecting a baby through the power of God. For nothing is impossible to God.' Mary said, 'Here I am, the servant of God. Let God's will be done in me.' Then Gabriel left her.

SONG	*'Hail Mary, gentle woman' by Carey Landry.*

The celebrant reads slowly, as in Lectio Divina. Allow time for people to enter into the meaning of the words. Allow pauses.

Celebrant	I invite you now to hear this reading again, but this time, imagine the angel is appearing to you where you are sitting right now. You would never expect an angel to come and speak to you! Now as I read again, hear your own name instead of the name 'Mary'. You might like to look at the picture of Mary you found on your seat when you came in. You see her open and listening, accepting the invitation she hears from God. Alternatively you might just like to close your eyes and picture the scene in your own mind.
	An angel appeared and said, 'Greetings, Mary. Greetings … (*Name*).

Repeat 'Greetings' a few times, naming someone in the congregation each time and allow a moment of silence for people to imagine hearing their own name.

Celebrant	God is really pleased with you. He is with you. Don't be afraid. For nothing is impossible to God.
	Yes, God tells you not to be afraid. God is really pleased with you. Blessed is that place in you where you said yes to God and where you allowed something of God to be born in you.
	God is born in you through the Holy Spirit and the power of God. For nothing is impossible to God.
	This is the word of the Lord.
All	**Thanks be to God.**
Celebrant	I invite you now to stand, and as you listen, open your hands like the image of Mary you found on your seats as you came in.
	Here I am, the servant of God. Let God's will be done in me.

Allow a moment of silence with everyone standing.

Celebrant	Do sit down again.

The celebrant offers a reflection based on the following questions:

Celebrant	• Who are the angels in my life?
	• How can I let God be born in me?
	Take some time now in silence to reflect on this. Now share any thoughts that came to you with a neighbour.

PRAYERS OF INTERCESSION

(Reword as you wish using simple words and short phrases.)

Celebrant	We give thanks for those who trust God.
	We pray to God's Holy Spirit to help each of us to say yes to God's call in my life.
	We pray for all the children here today including children yet unborn.
	We pray for expectant mothers.
	We pray for those who long for children.
	As we continue to pray I invite you to say a prayer out loud if you wish, from where you are sitting, closing it with 'Amen'. The rest of the congregation respond 'Amen' to each prayer. 'Amen' means 'Yes' just like Mary's 'Yes' to God.

This is when the people you have asked to be ready can say the prayer they prepared and when they also model saying 'Amen' after anyone else has prayed.

Celebrant	May we remember Lord, that with you, nothing is impossible.
	And may we be ready to play our part so that these prayers can be answered.

	And so we pray: Let it be done in me Lord according to your word.
All	**Let it be done in me Lord according to your word. Amen.**

OFFERTORY/COLLECTION

Take up the collection.

Celebrant   I invite you all to stand holding your hands open again as in the image of Mary, as we give thanks for the collection, and for the offering of our lives to God.

Celebrant prays.

All   **Amen.**

SENDING

Celebrant   Do take home the card with the image of Mary on it. You could place it in a prayer corner of your home and during the week when it catches your eye, think of Mary saying 'Yes' to God.

4   The Visitation

This service could be used if there is going to be an important meeting of two different groups or parishes.

Possible themes

Solidarity – recognition of God present in another person – confirmation of God's promise – rejoicing.

You will need

Actors

Mary – blue shawl.
Elizabeth – a shawl.

Preparation

- Rehearse the acting out of the story.
- Ensure there is someone to read the intercessions.
- Prepare large images of life-giving encounters, joyful, happy meetings (from the news, from the community of your own church).
- Make enough A8 cards for one per person of the image of the Visitation *(see above)* on one side, and on the other, the quotation 'Happy are you because you believed what God promised to you'.

Decoration

Project the image of the Visitation in the church, or display it at the entrance so people see it as they come in.

THE WORD Luke 1.39–45

Read the whole story from the Bible, or read the simplified version below:

Narrator
Mary was pregnant. She was expecting a baby whom she would call Jesus. He is the son of God. She felt very alone and so decided to visit her cousin, Elizabeth. The angel Gabriel had told her that although Elizabeth was too old to have children, she was expecting a baby, because nothing is impossible to God.

When Mary arrived in Elizabeth's home, Elizabeth's baby jumped in her womb. Elizabeth was filled with the Holy Spirit. Full of joy, she said, 'You are blessed by God, and the baby you are expecting is blessed too! How come the mother of my God is visiting me? Happy are you because you believed what God promised to you!' Mary was so full of joy she began singing praises to God.

Repeat the story as it is acted out:

Narrator
Mary was expecting a baby and felt very alone. She needed re-assurance from someone she loved and trusted so she left her home and went to visit her cousin, Elizabeth, who was also expecting a baby.

Mary is at the front of the church and walks from one side to the other where Elizabeth is waiting.

Narrator
When Mary and Elizabeth see each other, Elizabeth recognizes that Mary is carrying a baby inside her, and that the baby is God.

Mary and Elizabeth hug each other joyfully.

SONG
A version of the 'Magnificat' known and loved in your church or learn a new one, e.g. the 'Magnificat' (Mary's song) by Peter Kearney from his CD 'How far to Bethlehem?' (see Songs Appendix).

Narrator
Elizabeth was so full of joy she told Mary that she was blessed by God, and the baby she was expecting was also blessed.

Mary and Elizabeth freeze as a living icon in a mutual embrace.

The Celebrant offers a reflection on the Visitation as a model for all our relationships:

Celebrant
That God present in my heart recognizes God present in your heart.

That in all our meetings Jesus is present because he is present in our hearts.

That we all need people alongside us to give reassurance, encouragement and companionship in solidarity when we feel anxious and lonely.

That when we feel a call from God in our lives, we need a confirming sign from God.

That we need that call to be affirmed by someone we love and trust.

SONG   *'Tell out my soul the greatness of the Lord' by Timothy Dudley-Smith.*

Narrator   Mary stayed for three months with Elizabeth. God had given each of them a special job to do. They helped each other and supported each other as they prepared for their babies to be born.

Mary and Elizabeth stand together joyfully holding hands in mutual support.

Narrator   At the end of three months Mary returned home and soon after Elizabeth gave birth to a boy who was called John.

Mary goes back to the other side of the church where she came from initially. Elizabeth goes off in the opposite direction.

EXCHANGE OF PEACE

Celebrant   In Indian churches the peace is shared with a gesture known as 'Namaste'. The hands are folded together as if in prayer and each one bows to others who repeat the gesture to them. The gesture symbolizes 'God present in my heart, recognizes God present in your heart'.

This morning let us share the peace with each other using this gesture, reminding us of how Elizabeth recognized the presence of God in Mary, and inviting us to recognize the presence of God in each person we greet – and in ourselves too!

PRAYERS OF INTERCESSION

(Reword as you wish using simple words and short phrases.)

Celebrant   For those seeking a confirming sign from God in a time of doubt.
For those who are waiting to hear a word of consolation and affirmation from us.
For children yet to be born.
For expectant mothers.

For those who long to be mothers, but who are not able to have children.

For parents who are separated from their children for whatever reason.

OFFERTORY

A procession with:

- Bread.
- Wine.
- Large images of life-giving encounters, joyful, happy meetings (from the news, from the community of your own church).

SENDING

Give each person the small card with the image of the Visitation.

Celebrant   We have been thinking of the story of Mary and Elizabeth. Take home today the image of their meeting and each time you look at it this week, think of how we are all called to be Christ-bearers (Christophers!) and to support each other.

5   The Presentation of Jesus in the Temple

The Feast of the Presentation is also known as Candlemas. Traditionally celebrated on 2 February, but sometimes carried over to the nearest Sunday.

This service could be used to celebrate the birth of a child, or as a celebration of older people and their gifts of wisdom and experience, or for any intergenerational event, or when it occurs in the lectionary ...

Possible themes

Jesus as a light to the nations – God present in Jesus, each of us, therefore we are all called to be lights for the world – how our micro story reflects the macro story, i.e. we in some small way are Mary, or Joseph, or Anna, or Simeon.

You will need

Actors

Mary – choose someone who teaches in the Sunday school/children's liturgy group.
Joseph – choose a man with learning disabilities if possible.
Anna – choose an older woman who comes to church regularly for prayer times.
Simeon – choose an older 'wise' man.

Props

- A candle for each person in the congregation to be given out as people enter the church.
- A basket to hold the candles.
- The paschal candle or a large white candle to represent the light of Christ.
- A basket with the lid shut representing the basket carrying the two doves or pigeons.
- Shawls for Mary, Joseph, Anna and Simeon.
- Some coins.
- A8 cards in the shape of candles or with the image of a candle on them.

Preparation

- Rehearse Mary, Joseph, Anna, Simeon.
- Put out the cards with the image of a candle on them, and coloured pens for each row.

Decoration

Project the icon of the Presentation *(below)* or have it at the entrance so people see it as they come in.

THE GATHERING

Procession of the choir and celebrant, headed by Mary carrying the large candle and 'Joseph' carrying a basket representing the basket of two pigeons.

OR after the first hymn Mary and Joseph walk up the central aisle carrying the candle and pigeons.
Mary and Joseph go up to the front of the church where Simeon and Anna are standing on either side holding out their hands in a welcoming greeting.
Joseph lays the coins down before the altar.
Mary and Joseph sit in the congregation at the front.

OPENING PRAYER

Celebrant   O God who lives in Jesus, you welcome us into your church today just as you welcomed Jesus into the Temple in Jerusalem as a tiny baby.
You have planted your light in each human being. Whoever we are, each of us has our own unique light that comes from you.
You call us together today to follow in Jesus' footsteps and carefully carry the light that you have given us. We ask you to show us how to share the light that you have given us, and to honour the light of others in our church and neighbourhood, for your kingdom to grow here in …… (*Name of town*).

THE WORD Luke 2.22–38

Read the whole story from the Bible first, or read the simplified version below:

Narrator   Forty days after Jesus was born, Mary, his mother, and Joseph, her husband, took the baby to the Temple in Jerusalem to present him to God. The custom was to sacrifice two doves or pigeons, so Joseph took with him two birds.

Mary and Joseph go up to the front and are greeted by Simeon.

Narrator   There was a man in Jerusalem at that time called Simeon. He loved God and was faithful in prayer. The Holy Spirit had promised him he would not die before he had seen the Messiah, the chosen one of God. The Holy Spirit told him to go to the Temple on the day when Mary and Joseph came with their baby, Jesus. Simeon saw the baby, then took him in his arms.

Simeon takes the large candle and holds it high.

Narrator   He began to pray, praising God:

It would be good if Simeon could learn these lines. If not, he could read them. (If necessary, since he needs to hold the candle, someone could hold the reading for him.)

Simeon   Now, God, I can die in peace, just as you told me. I have seen with my own eyes how you will save your people. Now everyone can see your plan. This baby is the one who will be a light revealing God for all peoples in the world, showing your way to everyone. And he will bring glory to your people in Israel.

SONG   *A version of the 'Nunc Dimittis' the congregation know.*

Narrator   Mary and Joseph were astonished at his words.

Simeon hands the candle back to 'Mary'.

Narrator   Simeon blessed them and said to Mary:
Simeon   Many people in Israel will fall and many will rise because of this baby. He will be a sign from God that many people will not accept. The things they think in secret will be made known. And the things that will happen will make your heart sad, too – like a sword cutting into it.

SONG   *'Revealing the holy', by John Coleman.*

Reflection offered by the Celebrant:

Celebrant   How our lives reflect the lives of biblical characters:
- 'Mary' ...... *(Name)* gives birth to the word of God every week in the young people's liturgy.
- 'Joseph' ...... *(Name)* who cares for others.
- 'Simeon' ...... *(Name)* shares his wisdom with us.
- 'Anna' ...... *(Name)* may not be in church night and day, but is here praying every morning (or evening, or Sunday) faithfully.
- Which person from the Bible are we like?

I invite you to take some time now to think about what light God is asking you to bring to the world this week, or in your life in general. What is the gift God has given you that you can share with others? Then either write or draw this gift on the card you found on your seat as you came in. You will see there is an image of a candle on it, representing the light of Jesus in our lives.

Allow some time for this activity. Maybe play some gentle music in the background.

Narrator   You can choose whether to offer these cards in the collection plate, or to keep them with you to take home for your prayer corner.

PRAYERS OF INTERCESSION

(Reword as you wish using simple words and short phrases.)
These could be read by Mary and Joseph or by Anna and Simeon.

For those who give birth to Jesus today as Mary did 2,000 years ago.
For those who care for others as Joseph did.
For those who share their wisdom with us today as Simeon did.
For those who pray faithfully for others as Anna did.

For each prayer, appropriate and relevant examples could be given.

We pray for each of us to see God in our own lives.
We pray for each of us to see God in each other in this congregation.
We pray for each of us to see God in our neighbours in our town.
We pray for each of us to see God in our world in difficult situations of pain.

God of hopeful light: Jesus came to share your light with us, so that we can walk together in hope. Today, we pray for each of us to see your light bringing hope where it is most needed in our own lives.
God of hopeful light: Jesus came to be the light of your kingdom. Today, we pray for each of us in this congregation to see and rejoice in the light that you have planted in the heart of each person.
God of hopeful light: Jesus came bringing your light and your peace to our world.
We pray for our town, for all who live by your light, and work for your peace. We pray for us to all work together so that our town is a living sign of your kingdom of light and peace.
God of hopeful light: We pray especially for anyone going through a time of particular darkness, worry and pain, for whatever reason. We pray for the gift of courage to carry the candle of your light into the dark, bringing your hope, listening and encouragement to each one.

OFFERTORY

A procession including:

- The collection.
- Joseph offering the basket representing a basket of doves or pigeons.
- The coloured-in prayer card with the image of a candle, i.e. Jesus as the light of the world (unless people decide to take them home).
- What has been made in the Sunday school, e.g. a poster representing the light of Jesus shining in the midst of the darkness of our world. This can be created out of newspaper images of places suffering in the world, with an image of a candle in the centre representing Jesus as the light of the world.
- Bread.
- Wine.

EXCHANGE OF PEACE

Celebrant   In Indian churches the peace is shared with a gesture known as 'Namaste'. The hands are folded together as if in prayer and each one bows to others who repeat the gesture to them. The gesture symbolizes 'God present in my heart recognizes God present in your heart'.
This morning let us share the peace with each other using this gesture to remind us of how Simeon and Anna recognized God in the baby Jesus.

SENDING

During the final hymn Mary walks down the central aisle from the altar or communion table to the back of the church accompanied by Joseph.
Each person lights his or her candle from Mary's.
Then all turn and face the back of the church, the door to the outside where we are called to go and be lights in the world.

Celebrant   God of Light, you have shared your light with us in Jesus. I invite you to hold up your candles now and to see the light that fills the church now.
With Jesus, we have all we need to fulfil the unique mission you ask us to fulfil this week.
Send us out from here to the people and places that most need your light, so that we can bring your light and your hope to all those we meet, especially those most in need this week.

6   The wedding at Cana

This service could be used for celebrations of thanksgiving.

Possible themes

The abundant gifts of God – the kingdom of heaven being like a wedding feast – the transforming power of Christ – from loss to abundance – God's overflowing generosity.

You will need

Actors

Mary – shawl.
Jesus – white cloth.
Some disciples – coloured cloths.
A group to dance with a wedding couple – garlands.
Some servants – white aprons.
A steward – white apron and a belt made of a coloured cloth.

Some people to be representatives of the congregation, e.g. a child, an elderly person, a man, a woman, a person with a disability.

Props

- Six pots – the largest you can find or borrow.
- Jugs of water which can be poured into the pots.
- Ladle to take water out of the pots.
- Wine glass and blackcurrant juice for chief steward.
- A large container with a pot, jug or bowl in the centre of it.
- An attractive container filled with water by the side of it.
- An attractive glass to take water from the container and pour it into the vessel in the centre of the large container.
- Clean, empty jam jars with lids – one per household.

Preparation

- Rehearse the mimes.
- Teach a group of people the Israeli wedding dance using the tune: *Nigun Atik*.[5] Have a 'wedding' couple who go into the centre when the circle dances in and out of the centre. The raised hands of the people in the circle 'shower blessings' on the couple in the centre.
- Choose some representatives of the congregation and explain to them what they need to do (see below at the time of the Intercessions).
- Print enough A8 cards for one per person, with an image of the pot *(see p. 61)* on one side, and on the other, the quotation 'Do whatever he tells you' (John 2.5).

Decoration

- Project the image of the pot in the church – or display it at the entrance so people see it as they come in.
- Have large clay pots near the altar/communion table.

THE WORD John 2.1–11

Read the whole story from the Bible first, or just read the simplified version below:

Narrator   Jesus, his mother, Mary, and his friends were invited to a wedding in a town called Cana. Everyone was celebrating, having a good time drinking and dancing.

A group of people dance the Israeli wedding dance with a couple being blessed in the centre.

Narrator   Then there was no more wine!

Dancers look disappointed.

Narrator   Mary said to her son, Jesus, 'There is no more wine.'

Mary goes to Jesus and points to the empty pots.

Narrator   Jesus said, 'What's that got to do with me? It's not my time yet.' But his mother turned to the servants and told them, 'Do whatever he tells you.'

Mary turns to the servants and gestures to Jesus.

Narrator   Jesus said to the servants, 'Fill those six pots that are for washing with water, right up to the top.'

The servants look surprised, then pour water into the pots. They then look at Jesus and make gestures as if to say, 'And now what?!'

Narrator   Then Jesus said, 'Now take some out and give it to the chief steward.' So the servants took some out and gave it to the chief steward.

A servant ladles out some water into a wine glass (with his back to the congregation so they do not see that the glass has some blackcurrant juice already in it) and then gives it to the chief steward who drinks it.

Narrator   The chief steward drank the water that had become wine.

The chief steward drinks from the glass and looks astonished and delighted.

Narrator   He said to the bridegroom, 'People normally serve the best wine first, but you have kept the best till now, after the poorer wine has been drunk.'

The chief steward goes to the bridegroom and shows him his glass.
The dance is repeated and the dancers invite people from the congregation to join them. All look joyful.
The music stops and everyone freezes.

Narrator   This was the first miracle of Jesus. He showed his power by changing water into wine, and his friends now believed in him.

The friends of Jesus look with surprise at the pots, then at the chief steward's wine glass, then look in awe at Jesus. They kneel before him. All freeze for a few moments in silence.
Celebrant offers a reflection on the fact that Jesus came to give us life, and life to the full (John 10.10):

Celebrant   Jesus promises us streams of life-giving waters.
He enjoyed celebrations! He gives in abundance!

PRAYERS OF INTERCESSION

(Reword as you wish using simple words and short phrases.)

Celebrant   We pray for all those who find it hard to trust God.
              We pray for the relationships between parents and children, that
              the parents give their children the confidence and trust in God they
              need in life.
              We pray for those who find it hard to celebrate, for those who feel
              left out of celebrations, for them to know they are precious to God.
              We pray for our church, that we keep opening ourselves to the
              ways that God wants to reveal himself to us today.

OFFERTORY

*Along with the bread and wine offer clear glass jugs of grape juice to represent the
abundance of wine.*

Celebrant   Before the service started I asked some people to help me. Could
              they please come forward now?

The people asked come forward.

Celebrant   These people represent all of us. I'm going to ask them now to take
              turns to take some water from this container and to pour it into the
              container in the centre of this bowl.

*At the front have a large shallow container with a pot, bowl or jug in the centre of
it. By the side have a container of water. The people take it in turns to take water
and pour it into the container in the centre of the bowl. They should keep going
until the water overflows. They could invite members of the congregation to take
a turn.*

SONG   *As the water is being poured, sing until the pot overflows:*
              'Fill my cup, let it overflow, let it overflow with love.'
              *(This could be sung meditatively or at a quick joyful pace. You
              could sing just the chorus or make up some appropriate words
              to the verses. A good example is to be found on YouTube: St
              Petersburg Songsters: 'Fill my cup, let it overflow.')*

Celebrant   Thank you Lord that you came to bring us life, and life to the full,
              life that overflows! Amen.

COMMUNION

To be said at the appropriate point in the service:

Celebrant   By the mystery of this water and wine, may we come to share in the divinity of Christ, who humbled himself to share in our humanity.

Take a drop of water from the clay pot to mix with the wine for communion.

SENDING

Celebrant blesses the pot of water.

Celebrant   May you have life, and life to the full, life that overflows! Amen.

Invite people to stay for wine, soft drinks and nibbles.
Give people small glass jars (or one per family) and invite them to go and fill them with some of the blessed water. As they take the water have some people give out to each person the laminated A8 cards with the image of pots and the verse: 'His mother said to the servants, "Do whatever he tells you."' (John 2.5) on the other side.

7   The Samaritan woman

This could be used for services of peace and reconciliation, for gatherings of people from different cultures ...

Possible themes

Jesus' acceptance of the most rejected and despised of people – his offer of 'living water', of life to the full.

You will need

Actors

Narrator 1 (for the words of Jesus) – a man.
Narrator 2 (for the words of the Samaritan woman) – a woman.
Jesus – white cloth.

The Samaritan woman – shawl.
Disciples – coloured cloths worn like a stole.
Villagers – brown cloths, or normal clothes.

Props

- A well with cloths representing water.
- A water pot (as traditional as possible).
- Strips of blue cloth: enough for one each.
- A8 cards, enough for one per person with the photo of the woman going to the well on one side, and on the other, the quotation, 'I will give you living water' (John 4.10).
- A basket for the cards to be distributed.

Preparation

- Rehearse the actors.
- Scatter the cards and the strips of blue cloth on the water (blue cloths) overflowing from the well.

Decoration

- Project the photo of the woman going to the well *(see p. 66)* in the church, or display it at the entrance so people see it as they come in.
- Have a well in front of the altar, e.g. a large empty water drum covered by brown, grey or black cloths with long lengths of blue cloth, different shades, some white cloths cascading from it down the central aisle as water. Alternatively, a cheap blue storage tub with its handles cut off could be filled with water, and perhaps some submersible lights (from Glow Store), then decorated around the outside with fabric. Pile real rocks around it or draw stones on crumpled kraft paper. You could tuck ferns or ivy around too.
- A stool by the well for Jesus to sit on.

THE WORD John 4.1–30, 39–42

Read the whole story from the Bible first, or just read the simplified version below:

Narrator 1   Jesus was travelling back down to Galilee and had to pass through the country of Samaria. It was the middle of the day and very hot. Jesus was very tired and thirsty. He saw a well and sat down by it.

Jesus and some friends walk to the front. He sits by the well looking out at the congregation. The friends go off looking for food.

Narrator 2   Now most women go early to the well to fetch water so they can avoid the heat of the midday sun. They chat together. But that day one woman came at midday. She was alone. Maybe she wasn't liked by the other women.

The Samaritan woman carrying a water pot comes to the front centre from a different direction than Jesus.
Other women from the village gathered at the place the Samaritan woman came from, point at her as if gossiping about her and mocking her.

Narrator 1   Jesus asked her for a drink. His friends had gone to try and buy food.

Jesus raises a hand miming asking for water.

Narrator 2   The Samaritan woman was surprised he asked her for a drink as Jews like Jesus did not talk to Samaritans like her, and certainly not to a woman.

The Samaritan woman looks surprised.

Narrator 1   Jesus said to her, 'If you but knew the gift of God and who it is who is asking you for a drink, you would have asked him and he would give you living water.'

For the next part, Jesus and the Samaritan woman could freeze in position, as if they are talking with each other.

Narrator 2   The woman replied, 'You don't even have a bucket and this well is deep! Where are you going to get living water from?!'

Narrator 1   Jesus said, 'Everyone who drinks water from this well will get thirsty again. But anyone who drinks the water that I give will never be thirsty again. The water that I give will become in them a spring of water gushing up to never-ending life.'

Narrator 2   The woman asked, 'Sir, give me this water so I won't ever be thirsty again, and I won't have to keep coming here to fetch water.'

Narrator 1   Jesus asked her to call her husband and return with him.

Narrator 2   She said, 'I don't have a husband.'

Narrator 1   Jesus replied, 'You spoke the truth. You've had five husbands and the man you live with now is not your husband.'

Narrator 2   She said, 'You must be a prophet! So tell me, where should we pray to God?'

Narrator 1   Jesus said, 'Believe me, the time is coming and is already here, when true believers will not need a special place to worship God. They will worship him in spirit and in truth.

Narrator 2   The woman then said, 'I know the Messiah is coming. He will explain everything to us.'

Narrator 1   Jesus said, 'I am he, the Messiah.'
Just then his friends returned and were astonished that Jesus was talking with a Samaritan woman.

The friends return to Jesus and look surprised and shocked at him talking to the woman.

Narrator 2   As for the woman, she returned to her city and told everyone to come and see Jesus as she thought he might be the Messiah.

The woman runs off back where she came from and makes gestures for people to follow her, including the women who had mocked her, all the while pointing back at Jesus. She could do the same with some people from the congregation.

Narrator 2   She was so full of enthusiasm many returned with her and after listening to Jesus, believed in him, that he was the Messiah, the one sent by God.

People go with the woman to Jesus who welcomes them. They sit and listen to him intently.
The Celebrant offers a reflection on this encounter as a model for all our relationships:

Celebrant   Jesus is always there waiting for us, quietly, discreetly, without forcing himself on us.
The best way to help someone is often to ask them for help so they are no longer the beggar in need, but the one who can give.
Are we as free as the Samaritan woman to argue with Jesus, ask questions, listen to his replies and freely talk with him? He certainly responds!
Jesus affirms her for speaking the truth. Do we speak the truth with God, or do we first think we have to be good?
Notice that the one person Jesus tells that he is the Messiah is a woman, with a bad reputation, who is from a people seen as enemies by the Jews.

SONG   *'Come to the water' by John B. Foley.*
OR 'Let your living water flow over my soul, let your Holy Spirit come and take control' by John Watson.

PRAYERS OF INTERCESSION

Celebrant   We normally say some prayers of intercession. Today I invite you to simply sit in silence as if you are sitting by the well with Jesus. In your hearts, take time to speak truthfully to Jesus. Listen to what he might say to you in return. Have a conversation with Jesus, a heart to heart. We will take a few minutes for this. Ask Jesus your questions. Ask him for what you need or want. Or simply sit in silence with him, enjoying his presence.

Allow some time for this. If it would help, play some meditative music.

OFFERTORY

As the offerings of money, bread and wine are received, the Celebrant could lift high a clear glass jug of water and pour the water into a bowl so all can hear the sound of the water and see it splashing down.

Celebrant   Jesus said, 'The water that I give will become in you a spring of water gushing up to never ending life.'

SENDING

Celebrant   I invite each of you to go to the well, and to take a card and a strip of blue cloth from the overflowing waters for yourself. As you look at them this week think of Jesus' promise to you, that he will give you living waters springing up to eternal life. But remember, to receive this water, first you need to take time with Jesus, you need to go to the well where Jesus is waiting for you. He is always waiting for you, and always ready to welcome you. Take time to sit with Jesus this week.

When have you heard the word of God and put it into practice? When have you loved your neighbour as yourself as the word of God tells us to do? When have you shared the riches of your life with others in need? When have you experienced joy that catches alight in a group? Think of examples.

e of silent reflection.

We can joyfully hear the word of God, and then take time to reflect on it, trying to live as God wants us to live. Then our lives overflow with love and a deep joy and hope. Other people are touched by our lives.

Lord, thank you for those times when we live as you want us to live, loving others and delighting in your gifts to us.

Amen.

OF INTERCESSION

s you wish using simple words and short phrases.)

We pray for God to deepen our love for his word in our hearts, and to show us how his word is a constant source of hope in our daily lives.

Each of us may be the only Gospel that another person may 'read' today: we pray that our lives are true reflections of God's word, and that we are open to the invitations God gives us, to share his word in our daily lives.

We pray for each of the churches in our locality, that together we bear witness to Christ the sower, and support each other, as brothers and sisters in God's family.

We pray for anyone who is persecuted on account of the Gospel; we thank God for their example, and pray for the courage to keep fast to the faith in the face of our own challenges.

We pray for all those for whom faith appears impossible, who are each part of God's wider family.

8   The Parable of the Sower

This could be used for the beginning of an academic year, for listening to the word, for being willing to learn, or to challenge a congregation to be more receptive …

Theme

The importance of listening to what God says to each one of us, and the need to put that into practice for the good of the world.

You will need

Actors

A farmer – brown cloth as a stole.
Four people (A, B, C and D) to receive the 'word', each seated on a chair at the front – each with a green cloth round their shoulders. D needs to be confident to sing.
One person, dressed in bright colours, to dance to music.
Four people, dressed in black, to menace a seated person.
Two people, holding money and jewellery, to entice with riches a seated person.

Props

- 3 bowls, one of soil, one of seeds and one of seeds that have already started to grow.
- A bag of seeds.

- 2 mobile phones and 2 sets of headphones.
- Money, jewellery.

Preparation

- Rehearse the actors.
- Enough small packets of seeds for each one, or for each family. Each packet to have on it the words: 'Hear the word, accept it and bear fruit.'
- A basket for the packets of seeds.

Decoration

- A the entrance have three bowls, one of soil, one of seeds and one of seeds that have already started to grow so people see them as they come in.
- Project the image of the sower in the church, or have it displayed at the entrance.

THE WORD Mark 4.1–9, 13–20

Narrator   There was once a farmer who sowed seeds hoping for a good harvest when the seeds grew.

A farmer sows seed – by putting seeds one at a time into the outstretched palms of A, B, C and D sitting on chairs at the front and smiling. They receive the seeds joyfully.
B, C and D interact with A, as if chatting with him.

Narrator   Some seeds fell onto the path and the birds ate them up.

One person with headphones on comes forward and calls A with their mobile. A lets the seeds fall onto the ground and turns their back on the others; answers their phone and puts head phones on. A continues to mime chatting on their mobile.

Celebrant   What are your distractions from putting the word of God into practice in your lives?

Allow a time of silent reflection.

Celebrant   God sows the word in our hearts and very quickly we can be distracted by voices other than God and the seed disappears.
Lord, help us to stay centred on you and not be distracted by other things.

All   **Amen.**

Narrator   Some seeds fell onto rocky ground where there was little soil so they could not put down roots. The seeds grew quickly but then withered and died under the hot sun because they did not have good roots.

C and D interact with B, as if chatting, wanting
Four people come behind the B and repeatedly a
    'Where's that report?!'
    'Where's your rent?!'
    'I'm leaving you!'
    'You're not good enough!'
B looks fearful and drops the seeds, crumpling
completely crouched over, blocking out the voice
they go making menacing gestures.

Celebrant   What troubles make you fall av
            you to do?

Allow a time of silent reflection.

Celebrant   We can joyfully hear the word (
            fearful that we no longer nourish
            troubles and not of God's helping
            Lord, when troubles come and we
            and not be fearful.
All   **Amen.**
Narrator   Some seeds fell among thorns wh
            be no harvest.

D tries to interact with C.
Two people come near C and hold out money and
C turns eagerly to take the money and jewellery ar
laughing. C dresses up with the jewellery and rema

Celebrant   What temptations fill your life lea
            desires do you have that make you

Allow a time of silent reflection.

Celebrant   We can joyfully hear the word of C
            many things – money, power, riches
            by all our wealth and turn away fro
            Lord, help us not to be tempted by
            you.
All   **Amen.**
Narrator   Some seeds fell on good soil. They g

D picks up the large image of a field of corn (see p.
image joyfully; then begins to sing, 'Rejoice in the
then invites everyone to sing as well.
A, B, and C look surprised.
The celebrant encourages a few people to join in
everyone.

Celebrant

Allow a tin
Celebrant

All

PRAYERS

(Reword

Celebrant

OFFERTORY

A procession of:

- The collection.
- Bread.
- Wine.
- The three bowls: of earth, of seeds, of growing seeds.

SONG   *The offertory hymn, which could be 'All good gifts around us'. The Godspell version could be learned.*

Celebrant   I invite you all to stand now and to stretch out your hands to the front as a sign of offering the word we have received this morning.

Celebrant gives thanks and blesses the offerings.

Celebrant   Now I invite you to turn your hands over and to place them on the shoulders of someone in front of you as a blessing. Any gift we receive from God is always for the good of others. So let us now in a moment of silence, pray for the person in front of you.

A song of blessing could be sung.

SENDING

Celebrant   As you leave I invite you to take a packet of seeds. You will see on it the words, 'Hear the word, accept it and bear fruit'. So now go out into the world and listen to the word of God this week, accept it and bear fruit.

The person who played the fourth seated person could be the one who gives out the packets of seeds.

9   The Feeding of the 5,000

*This could be used at harvest time, or
when there are special collections for
a major charity to encourage people
to contribute what they can, or for an
ecological service to emphasize that
nothing is wasted, or when the aim
is to encourage the hidden talents of
children or people with disabilities.*

Possible themes

Trust in God's providence – believing that with God we can make a
difference – abundance from scarcity
– nothing is wasted.

You will need

Actors

Jesus – white cloth.
Peter – brown cloth.
Disciples – dark coloured/multicoloured cloths.
Little boy – rough material.

Props

- Twelve baskets.
- Five loaves of bread.
- Two fish (could be cut out of card and painted).

Preparation

- Rehearse the actors.
- Cut out paper or card shapes of fish and loaves of bread *(see Appendix 5)*.
- Make A8 cards, enough for one per person, with the image of the feeding of the 5,000 (or an image of five loaves and two fish) on one side, and on the other, the quotation 'There was enough for all'.

Decoration

Project the image of the feeding of the 5,000 in the church – or display it at entrance so people see it as they come in.

GATHERING

Give out paper or pieces of card cut out in the shape of loaves or fish so that people have 'food' ready for later in the service.

THE WORD Mark 6.34–44 or John 6.1–15

Narrator   Jesus and his disciples came to a lonely place but he saw that a large crowd had already gathered to listen to him. He took pity on them because they looked like lost sheep without a shepherd.

Jesus and the disciples come in and see the crowds (the congregation).
The little boy must sit in the centre of the congregation.

Narrator   He began to teach them. He told them the good news:
that they were loved by God who is our Father,
that the kingdom of heaven was close at hand,
that the poor were blessed,
that God had a special love for the poor,
that we have to become like little children who trust in order to enter the kingdom of heaven.
And all day the crowd listened because he had lived the beatitudes for 30 years himself before ever speaking about them and so he

taught them with authority in a way that made them listen to every word he said.

Jesus faces everyone and gestures at the congregation as if teaching them.

Narrator   But then the sun began to set. It was late and everyone was tired. The people were hungry!

Jesus gestures to the congregation, the crowd, who look hungry. Jesus looks concerned and sad.

Narrator   The friends of Jesus told him to send the crowd away so they could find something to eat.

The disciples make appropriate gestures.

Narrator   But Jesus told them to feed the people themselves.

Jesus gestures appropriately.

Narrator   The friends of Jesus protested they didn't have enough money to buy that amount of food. They thought Jesus was a little unrealistic!

The disciples show empty pockets and hands.

Narrator   But Jesus said, 'Go and see what food there is.'

Jesus points to the crowd.

Narrator   So the disciples went into the crowd asking who had any food.

The disciples go into the congregation to see who has food.

Narrator   No one gave anything. Then one little boy piped up and said, 'I have five barley loaves and two fish.'

The little boy stands up from the centre of the church and holds out his food, the five loaves and the two paper or card fish.

Narrator   But Peter said, 'That is nothing for so many!'

Jesus shakes his head at Peter.

Narrator   Jesus, though, smiled at the little boy.
He told the people to sit down in groups.
He took the bread and the fish.
He gave thanks for the food.
He broke the bread,
and then gave the bread and the fish to his friends to give out to the waiting crowd.

Jesus makes appropriate gestures as the above lines are read out.
The disciples then give out the five loaves to the congregation while the following song is sung.

SONG   'Be still for the presence of the Lord' by David Evans.

Narrator   There was enough for all! Everyone ate and was satisfied!
                    Jesus then told the disciples to collect the scraps that were left so
                    that nothing would be wasted.

The disciples collect the baskets with the remaining crumbs and bring them back to Jesus.

Narrator   There were twelve baskets full of scraps!
                    Seeing this, the crowds said, 'This is indeed the prophet of God
                    who is to come into the world!'

Jesus kneels and prays in thanksgiving.

PRAYERS OF INTERCESSION

Celebrant   Jesus sent the crowds away and went off into the hills to pray. We
                    are now going to take time to pray ourselves. That day the people
                    were hungry and were fed. What is your hunger today? I invite you
                    now to draw or write your needs on the slips of paper in the shape
                    of loaves or fish which you were given as you came in.

Allow a few minutes for this.

Celebrant   If you are happy for me to read out your prayer could you now
                    put your cards in the baskets that are being passed round? If you
                    prefer, you could keep the cards and use them during your prayer
                    time at home this week.

Collect the baskets and hand to the celebrant who could read some of the prayers out. Invite everyone to reply 'Amen' to each prayer.

OFFERTORY

Offer up the baskets of prayers along with the bread and wine for communion, and the baskets with the remaining crumbs of bread and the two fish.

Celebrant   As we offer our gifts of money and our prayers, we offer also ourselves, trusting that just as Jesus took the bread, blessed it, broke it and gave it, so he can do the same with our lives. He takes the broken bits of our lives, blesses us, so we can give life to others. So let's sing now 'Spirit of the living God fall afresh on me' (Daniel Iverson), but we will slightly change the words:

SONG   *'Spirit of the living God, fall afresh on me' (x 2)*
Take me, break me, bless me, use me.
Spirit of the living God, fall afresh on me.

SENDING

Celebrant   Take home the cards with the image of the feeding of the 5,000 (or an image of five loaves and two fish). The words, 'There was enough for all' on the back, are a reminder for you this week of God's invitation for each of us to give what we can, and then to trust that God can multiply our gifts a hundredfold.
I invite you to be aware of the needs locally, in our own church and neighbourhood, and then to bring, as the little boy did, some food you feel able to offer for a food bank next week.

10   The Raising of Lazarus

This could be used before Holy Week, or for any celebration of hope in times of sorrow or despair.

Theme

From death to life – belief in the midst of grief and loss – celebration of life over that which destroys – being freed.

You will need

Actors

Jesus – a white cloth round his shoulders, or a white cassock.
Martha – a shawl.
Mary – a shawl.
Lazarus – a white cloth wrapped tightly around him.
A messenger.
Disciples – coloured cloths round their shoulders.
Mourners/the tomb (enough people to form a circle round Lazarus lying on the floor) – black cloths round their shoulders.

Props

- Stones in a large basket at the entrance.
- There could be one very long black cloth to be held in a circle around Lazarus by the mourners making the tomb.
- Baskets to collect the stones.

Preparation

- Rehearse the actors. If an actor cannot say their lines then the narrator can say them instead. In which case each time the narrator needs to say 'Jesus said ...' or 'Martha said ...' etc.
- Choose some meditative sad instrumental music.
- If time permits in the service, ask someone beforehand to prepare to share about a time of grieving they have gone through.

Decoration

- Project the icon of Lazarus *(see p. 81)* in the church, or display it at the entrance so people see it as they enter for the service.
- Give a stone to each person as they arrive.

THE WORD (from John 11)

SONG   *'Never give up (Bambelela)', a traditional South African song by John Bell. Sing quietly and sadly.*

Narrator   Jesus loved two sisters called Mary and Martha, and their brother, Lazarus. They were at home in Bethany. Lazarus, their brother was seriously sick.

Mary and Martha stand on one side at the front as if at home in Bethany. They bend over Lazarus who is clearly very ill.

Narrator   Mary and Martha sent a message to Jesus telling him that Lazarus was sick and asking him to come.

On the other side at the front stand Jesus and his disciples. Jesus mimes teaching them. A messenger is sent by Mary and goes from Bethany to Jesus.

Narrator   Jesus refused to go to Lazarus.

Jesus raises his hand as if saying 'No' to the messenger.

Narrator   He said the sickness of Lazarus was for the glory of God.

Jesus raises his hand to point up to God and smiles.

Narrator   Lazarus died and his sisters wept in grief for him. They were deeply upset that Jesus had refused to come to heal their brother and that Lazarus had died.

Martha covers Lazarus with a white cloth. The sisters bend over his body and weep. Men with black cloth round their shoulders carry Lazarus to the centre at the front, then form a circle round him lying on the floor making a tomb with their bodies and the long black cloth.

Narrator   Turn to a person sitting next to you and take some time now to reflect on what the sisters would have been thinking and sharing. What were their memories of Jesus? How was it to welcome him into their home, to listen to him, to enjoy his friendship? How might they feel that he does not come now when they need him the most? How might Martha respond? By keeping the home going with food and so on? How might Mary respond? By sitting silently on her own, grieving?

Take some time now to reflect on times when you personally have felt alone, abandoned, full of grief, or were angry with God. How did you feel, how did you react? As you reflect, look at your stone. Feel it in your hands: the hardness of it, the weight, the coldness.

Allow some time for this and during this time play some meditative, sad, instrumental music.

SONG   *'Miseri mei domine, miserere', Taizé chant.*

If time permits, a person could be asked to talk about a time of grieving they went through. If so, repeat the Taizé chant afterwards.

Narrator   After four days Jesus finally went to Bethany.

Jesus walks across to Bethany but stops midway between the tomb and where he has come from. Before he reaches the family, Martha runs to him.

Martha   If only you had come, my brother would still be alive!

If time permits, the same person talks about the experience of holding onto faith even in the midst of grieving.

Celebrant   I invite you now to take a few moments to reflect on how you hold onto hope in the midst of difficulties and grieving, how you hold onto faith even though God does not seem to be listening to you.

Allow a time of silence for this.

SONG   *The chorus, 'Kyrie eleison, Christe eleison, Kyrie eleison' from the song 'Look around you, can you see?' by Jodi Page-Clark.*

Jesus	I am the resurrection. If anyone believes in me, even though he dies, he will live. Whoever lives and believes in me, will never die. Do you believe this?
Martha	I believe.
Narrator	Mary came running to him.

Mary runs to Jesus.

Mary	If only you had come, my brother would still be alive!

SONG	*The chorus, 'Kyrie eleison, Christe eleison, Kyrie eleison' from the song: 'Look around you, can you see?'*

Narrator	Jesus wept.

Jesus weeps.

Celebrant	Let us now take a few moments to pray in silence for those places today where Jesus weeps, for those people who suffer and for whom Jesus weeps. As we pray, feel the stone you were given; look at it. Stones can be hard, cold, heavy. Grief can feel hard, cold, heavy. Anyone who would like to, just say one word naming out loud a place of suffering or a person who is grieving.

Allow time for this.

SONG	*'Look around you, can you see?' by Jodi Page-Clark.*

Narrator	Then Jesus went to the tomb.

Jesus goes to tomb.

Narrator	We have been thinking of times we have felt dead, but we can also keep ourselves entombed. Would some people be willing to come forward to become some of the stones entombing Lazarus?

The people stand around the tomb as stones (if people come forward who are not actors, give them a black cloth and guide them as to what to do).

Narrator	Jesus said,
Jesus	Take the stone away! Lazarus – come out! Unbind him. Let him go free!

The 'stones' release as Lazarus stands up and comes forward.

SONG	*'Behold, behold, I make all things new' by John L. Bell.*

Narrator   Mary, Martha and Jesus went back to a meal in Bethany with Lazarus. We too can celebrate by sharing the bread of life (or traybakes if that is what will be used!) together now.

If the service is not one with Holy Communion, then some traybakes might be passed round now.

SONG   *'Never give up (Bambelela)' (This time sung joyfully and confidently.)*

PRAYERS OF INTERCESSION

(Reword as you wish using simple words and short phrases.)

Celebrant   We pray with those who have recently lost a loved one, in our own families, in the parish, and beyond.
We pray for any whose grief seems overwhelming and endless.
We pray to resist the temptation to give easy answers to anyone suffering, or in grief.
Help us to witness God's love for them through our simple presence.

SONG   *'Look around you, can you see?'* by Jodi Page-Clark.

OFFERTORY

Collect the stones into a basket at the same time as the collection is taken, then bring them up to leave at the altar.
Take up the bread and wine.

SENDING

Celebrant   I invite you as you leave to come forward and take a stone from those that were brought up for the offertory. Each stone represents a sign of sharing someone else's grief. Because we know that Jesus rose from the dead we know he is with us. We do not have to carry a whole bag of grief alone. We can help each other by carrying some of the pain of another person.

11 The Call of Mary Magdalene

This could be used in the Easter season, or for someone being missioned, or to highlight the positive role of women in the gospel story.

Possible themes

Hope – being missioned – death to life.

You will need

Actors

Jesus – white cloth.
Mary Magdalene – shawl.
Peter – coloured cloth.
John – coloured cloth.
Two angels – white cloths.
Disciples – coloured cloths.

Props

- A life-size cross (one can be made of lightweight thin pinewood and painted black).
- Black cloth hung to represent the tomb.
- Bench inside the tomb.
- White grave cloths folded, one small one, others next to it on the bench inside the tomb.
- Vases of flowers in tomb.

- Little bells.
- Slips of paper, one for each person, and coloured pens.
- Candles, enough for one each per household.

Preparation

- Rehearse the actors.
- Print enough A8 cards for one per person of the icon of Mary Magdalene in the garden on one side, and on the other, the quotation: *'Risen Jesus, bless our home with your love.'*
- Cover the cross used on Good Friday with flowers (if this liturgy is used for Easter Sunday).

Decoration

- Project in the church the icon of Mary Magdalene meeting Jesus in the garden, or display it at the entrance so people see it as they come in.
- Have incense burning or use essential oils so people enter to the 'perfume' of the resurrection.
- At the front hang a black cloth to represent the tomb. One simple way is to hang a line like a washing line and use safety pins to attach the cloth to the line. The cloth could be looped up to show the tomb is open. Inside there should be a bench with white grave cloths folded on it. The angels can sit at either end of the bench. There could be vases of flowers around the tomb entrance but make sure there is space for actors to enter.
- The cross covered with flowers could be placed nearby.

GATHERING

As people arrive offer them little bells to ring at appropriate points in the service. Invite people to write their name clearly on a slip of paper.

THE WORD John 20.1–18

Celebrant   Jesus was buried in the tomb on Friday, the women waited all day Saturday and then on Sunday morning – where were the women? They came to show their love for Jesus by anointing his body with spices. Here we are too, come to show our love ...

SONG   *'Ubi caritas'*, Taizé chant.

MIME

The tomb is open, two angels sit on the bench inside, one at each end.
Disciples at one side.
Mary at the back of the church.
Jesus hidden on the other side to the disciples.

Narrator	Early on the first day of the week when it was still dark, Mary Magdalene came to the tomb. She saw that the stone had been moved away from the tomb and came running to Peter and the disciple that Jesus loved. She cried out, 'They have taken the Lord out of the tomb and we don't know where they have put him.'

Mary goes from the back of the church, up the central aisle, to the tomb at the front carrying burning spices/incense. She sees the tomb is open, and runs to the disciples.

Narrator	So Peter and the disciple Jesus loved ran to the tomb but the disciple Jesus loved was faster and reached the tomb first. He bent down and looked in and saw the white grave cloths lying there but he did not go in.

John runs fast to the tomb and looks in. Peter follows more slowly.

Narrator	When Peter reached the tomb he went inside and saw the cloths, and also the cloth that had covered the head of Jesus.

Peter reaches the tomb and goes inside.

Narrator	Then the other disciple went inside; he saw, and he believed.

John goes inside.

Narrator	Then they went home, leaving Mary alone in the garden.

Peter and John return to their home. Mary stays weeping where she is.

Narrator	Mary stood there weeping. Then she too looked inside the tomb and saw two angels in white sitting where the body of Jesus had been, one at the head and one at the feet.

Mary looks inside the tomb and sees the two angels.

Narrator	The angels said to her, 'Woman, why are you weeping?' She said to them, 'They have taken my Lord away and I don't know where they have laid him.' As she said this she turned round and saw Jesus standing there, though she didn't recognize him because of her tears.

Jesus comes to stand just behind Mary. Mary weeping, turns around and sees Jesus.

| Narrator | Jesus said to her, 'Woman, why are you weeping? Who are you looking for?' Thinking he was the gardener she said, 'Sir, if you have taken him away, tell me where you have put him, and I will go and remove him.'
Then Jesus said, 'Mary.' She replied 'Master.' |

Mary falls at the feet of Jesus and tries to touch them.

| Narrator | Jesus said to her, 'Do not hold onto me, because I have not yet gone up to the Father. But go to my friends and tell them: I am going up to my Father and your Father, to my God and your God.' |

Jesus points up to God in heaven.

| Narrator | So Mary Magdalene told the friends of Jesus, 'I have seen the Lord. He is risen from the dead. He is alive.' |

Mary runs back to the disciples in the upper room shouting the news. They look astounded, then slowly are full of joy.

| Mary | Jesus is risen from the dead! He is alive! |

Mary then comes to the centre at the front and tells the congregation:

| Mary | Jesus is risen! He is risen indeed! Alleluia! |
| Narrator | Jesus died. He has risen. He is risen indeed. Alleluia! |

Encourage everyone to respond: 'He is risen indeed! Alleluia!' and to ring their bells. Repeat as often as seems right.

| SONG | *Any joyful Easter song that is well known by the congregation.*
OR 'I saw Mary in the garden' by Rowland Howarth. |

PRAYERS OF INTERCESSION

Celebrant   We pray for peace in Jerusalem and the Middle East.

We pray for any who struggle to believe that Jesus truly did rise from the dead, and is alive and active with the life of God today in the church and the world.

We pray to be receptive to all those God chooses to bring his message of hope.

We pray for openness to see how each of us, like Mary, is called to be a witness of the resurrection and to take that message wherever God sends us.

We pray that we might be compassionate and loving, like Mary Magdalene, wanting to do what we can for those we love.

We pray for those who are blinded by grief.

May we be able to recognize the risen Jesus in our lives so that we can tell others of his love and not cling to the past.

We pray that we might be able to hear God calling us by name.

OFFERTORY

Celebrant   During the singing of the offertory hymn take some time to write your name on the slips of paper provided if you haven't already done so. You could draw yourself if you prefer. This is a symbol of your offering of yourself to the Jesus who knows you and calls you by name.

SONG   *The hymn 'Christ the Lord is risen today' by Charles Wesley.*

People offer their names, or their drawings, at the same time as their collection, as a symbol of offering themselves along with their money.
As part of the offertory procession, take up burning incense as Mary took spices to the tomb.

EXCHANGE OF PEACE

Celebrant   Ask your neighbour's name if you do not know it, then address them by name: ...... *(Name)*, the Lord is risen! And reply, ... *(Name)*, he is risen indeed!

COMMUNION

Where possible, probably only in smaller churches, the minister could name each person as they are given communion: ...... (Name) the body of Christ broken for you.

SENDING

Celebrant   Each person, household or family is now invited to come forward and light a candle from the Easter candle to take home as a sign of the light of Christ. Take the light of Christ home and say a blessing for each room in your house.

The following blessing could be suggested or small cards could be given out with the icon of Mary Magdalene in the garden on one side and the words: 'Risen Jesus, bless our home with your love' on the back.

Celebrant   You are also invited to take a flower from the cross to decorate your home. Let us wish each other a happy Easter and ring out the bells in celebration.

Ring the bells.

12   The Risen Jesus appearing by the lakeside

This could be used in the Easter season, or at dawn on Easter Sunday. If your church is by the sea or a lake the service could be on the shore.

Possible themes

Hope – Forgiveness and reconciliation.

You will need

Actors

Peter – a coloured cloth.
John – a coloured cloth.
Jesus – a white cloth or cassock.
Other disciples – coloured cloths.

Props

- Sea – blue cloth.
- Land – green cloth.
- A boat (a table on its side with blue cloth along the bottom for water. A simple picture of a boat drawn onto a large sheet of paper could be stuck on the table on its side or a Sunday school or youth group could make a boat out of a large cardboard box).
- A fishing net (fruit netting from a garden centre or just a bit of gauzy fabric).
- Life jackets for the disciples.
- Fish (painted, cut-out pieces of card in the shape of fish).
- Fire, e.g. a cluster of lit candles of different heights, bits of wood or logs, wood-shavings. OR put some logs together, either real logs or corrugated cardboard, then flames made with crêpe paper, scrunched up tissue, or you can get fancy and attach flame-coloured fabric flames to a fan that is placed on its side for real moving flames!
- Matches.
- A basket and a loaf of bread.
- A long black cloth to represent the night.
- The sun, e.g. a large circular card painted bright yellow or a large yellow ball.
- Bells, percussion instruments.

Preparation

- Rehearse the mime.
- Make the necessary props.
- Print A8 cards in the shape of a fish *(see image on the right, or Appendix 5)* with the words: *'Do you love me? Feed my sheep'* on the back (enough for one per person).

Decoration

- Project the image of 'It is the Lord' by Katharine Hall *(see p. 92)* in the church or display it at the entrance so people see it as they come in.
- Create the scene at the front of the church with a boat and blue cloth for sea (these can be laid down immediately in front of the first row in the church), and a fire on green cloth representing the land.
- Give people in the congregation the fish ready to throw into the net at the right time.

THE WORD John 21.1–19

Celebrant	On Palm Sunday we remembered how Jesus entered the city of Jerusalem – and all the crowds greeted him; on Thursday we remembered how he ate a meal with his friends and how he washed their feet. On Good Friday we remembered how he was killed on the cross. Easter Saturday was a quiet day. We remembered how Jesus lay in the grave, dead. On Easter Sunday many of us went to church and celebrated how Jesus rose from the dead. We heard the priest say, 'The Lord is risen', and we all replied, 'He is risen indeed! Alleluia!' But then what happened? It wasn't easy to believe – that someone could rise from the dead! that Jesus was really alive! And his friends felt lost and confused.

Three disciples – talk together, lost and sad.

Celebrant	So Peter said to some of Jesus' friends, John and James, 'I'm going fishing.' And they said, 'We'll come with you.'

Peter gestures to the other two disciples and they put life jackets on and get in the boat. All the while Jesus sits (on the green cloth for the land) and mimes making a fire (he could light the candles if that is how the fire is going to be made) while he watches the disciples.

Celebrant	When do we feel like this? Unable to believe that Jesus is risen...?

Allow some time for silent reflection, or for sharing with a neighbour.

SONG	*Kyrie eleison, Christe eleison, Kyrie eleison. (A version your church knows well)*

Celebrant	So Peter and the friends of Jesus went out onto the lake in a boat and fished all night.

Two people hold up a black cloth at the back to represent the night.
The disciples get in the boat and throw the net to one side.
Encourage the people in the front row to flutter the blue cloths laid in front of them creating waves.

Celebrant	But they caught nothing. As the sun began to rise,

The people holding the black night cloth slowly lower it, as a person carries the sun across the room and then stands behind Jesus holding the sun above him.

| Celebrant | they saw a man on the beach. It was Jesus. He called out, 'Have you caught anything?' They shouted back, 'No.'
Jesus said, 'Throw your net on the other side and you will catch fish.' |

The disciples throw the net to the other side.
Encourage the audience to throw the fish they were given earlier into the net.

| Celebrant | So they did this, and there were so many fish it was hard to pull the net in. |

The disciples haul the net in and are astounded by the number of fish.

| Celebrant | Can you remember times when everything seems hopeless, we do all we can, but nothing seems to work, we catch nothing? Then we need to remember to turn to Jesus, and things begin to come together. |

Allow some time for silent reflection, or for sharing with a neighbour.

| SONG | *Kyrie eleison, Christe eleison, Kyrie eleison.* |

| Celebrant | Then the friend Jesus loved said, 'It is the Lord!'
When he heard this, Peter jumped into the water and swam to Jesus. |

Jesus and Peter greet each other with joy, hugging each other if appropriate.

| Celebrant | The other friends of Jesus rowed the boat with all the fish to land. When they got there, they saw that Jesus had prepared a fire, and bread. He said, 'Bring some of your fish and come and eat!' |

The other disciples bring the boat to shore, then get out and go to Jesus looking full of wonder.

| Celebrant | Jesus took some bread, blessed it, gave thanks to God … |

Jesus raises the bread and looks up to heaven.

| Celebrant | … broke it and shared it with his friends. |

Jesus breaks the bread and shares it with the disciples.
They pass it round so everyone has a bit of bread.

| Celebrant | The celebrant could give a reflection on how Jesus feeds us, cares for us, loves us and longs to share his life with us. |

| SONG | *'Take this bread, eat this bread, eat, and never be hungry', Taizé chant.* |

Celebrant   Afterwards Jesus took Peter to the side and sat alone with him. He said to Peter, 'Do you love me?'

Jesus and Peter go to the side and sit facing each other.

For the following lines, either Jesus and Peter say the lines having learned them, or they make appropriate facial expressions and hand movements to the words of the narrator.

Celebrant   Peter said, 'Yes, Lord. You know I do.'
Jesus said, 'Feed my lambs.'
Jesus asked a second time, 'Do you love me?'
Peter said, 'Yes, Lord. You know I do.'
Jesus said, 'Feed my sheep.'
Jesus asked a third time, 'Do you love me?'
Peter said, 'Yes, Lord. You know I do.'
Jesus said, 'Feed my sheep.'
This was the third time that Jesus appeared to his friends after he rose from the dead. And today, he asks each one of us as he asked Peter: 'Do you love me?'
Then he asks us, as he asked Peter, to look after those in need, his lambs, his sheep.
What is our response?

Allow some time for silent reflection, or for sharing with a neighbour.

The celebrant could give a reflection on the story and what it says to their own church today.

Celebrant   The Lord is risen!
All   **He is risen indeed!**
                 Alleluia! (3 x)

SONG   *Easter songs! Ring bells, play percussion instruments.*

PRAYERS OF INTERCESSION

(Reword as you wish using simple words and short phrases.)

Celebrant   Forgive us for the times we carry on our normal lives as we have always done and forget you are alive and with us today.
Thank you for loving us even when we turn away from you.
Help us to hear your call to go and care for others, especially the weakest and those most in need.

OFFERTORY

Bring up:

- Bread and wine.
- The fishing net with the cut out cardboard fishes.

SENDING

Give people as they leave a card in the shape of a fish (see p. 93 or Appendix 5) with the words: 'Do you love me? Feed my sheep', on the back.

PART 4

How to plan creative inclusive small group celebrations

Introduction

A growing number of churches have discovered the benefits of setting up a small group whose specific aim is to support the members of their congregation with learning disabilities. Such groups often find it helpful to join a wider network, such as Faith and Light, which has many resources and creative ideas. Much of the know-how here draws on their expertise. Inclusion is at the heart of such groups. Faith and Light was founded not just so that people with learning disabilities could find their place at the heart of the church, but also so that family members could find support, and importantly, to make it easier for others to discover the gift of people with learning disabilities. Prospects (Livability) run similar groups. See the Appendixes for their websites.

Such groups soon develop a community feel, due to the common interest and activities of its different constituents: a balance between children, teenagers or adults with an intellectual disability, their family and friends, who meet together at least once a month for sharing, prayer and celebration, all in a spirit of mutual support and friendship.

In this section, we provide some useful guidelines for running such a group, as well as twelve themed celebrations for use at group gatherings.

Guidelines for planning
small group celebrations

Ideally, one week before a meeting send out an invitation to each member of the group reminding them of the date, time and place of the meeting. Mention the theme, and anything they might need to bring. Getting a personal invitation like this brings its own sense of dignity and joy! For Theresa in Chennai, the people in Faith and Light were her only friends outside her family and she eagerly awaited her monthly invitation.

Preparation

Set up the room the way you want it before the group arrives:

- The correct number of chairs arranged in a circle.
- A decoration related to the theme of the gathering as a focal point.
- Any materials for planned activities ready to hand.
- Space for group work, including the necessary materials.
- Refreshments available.

WELCOME

- A group member with learning disabilities could take on the responsibility of welcoming each person by name at the door as they arrive. This could be done together with a person without disabilities.
- Name badges with photos are useful as a sign of group membership; these could either be given out at each meeting, or kept by the group members. Keep a list of the group members. For health and safety it needs to be clear who is present and who is not. Follow up absentees. A phone-call to someone who did not come lets them know they were missed so they feel wanted and loved.
- Play some music as people arrive, to help people feel safe and focused.
- Once most have arrived, two people invite the others to sit in a circle.

- Welcome each person to the circle with a familiar song e.g. the Afro-American spiritual *'He's got the whole world in his hands'* (then substitute the name of each person in turn in the group for 'the whole world'). Songs in which people's names can be included become very popular. The group might end up singing the same welcome song each week! Theresa in Chennai certainly insisted on us singing, *'He's got the whole world in his hands ... He's got Theresa in his hands ...'*
- Keeping to the same format helps people to feel at home and more confident in the group. As they get used to the markers that indicate the various parts of the meeting, try inviting a person with learning disabilities to take on some aspect of leading the meeting.
- Invite people to share news since the last meeting. To keep good order, use a 'speaking symbol', e.g. a red heart-shaped cushion. Give this to the first person and invite them to begin. This person then chooses the next one to speak by calling that person's name and throwing the cushion to him or her.
- Stand to sing an action song, preferably one appropriate to the theme. Movement and fun bring people together, and help them relax.

ACTIVITY AND PRAYER *(see the 12 outline celebrations below)*

EXPLANATION OF THEME

- Introduce the theme of the evening in a simple way, outlining the programme. 'Our theme today is X, and what we will do is ...' This might need repeating a couple of times, so that each one is on board. Knowing what will happen helps lessen potential anxiety. It also helps to establish the ritual and reinforces the theme.
- Refer to the theme a few times while the group carries out the chosen activity.
- And, again, at the end, summarize the theme and remind the group of the activity: 'Today we thought about .../ made.../ heard a story about ...'

BREAKING OPEN THE WORD TOGETHER

- Place a Bible in the centre and explain this is a book that tells us the story of God's love for us. 'There are many stories in the Bible. Today we will think about .../ make .../ hear a story about ...'
- Light a candle, and place it on a saucer next to the Bible and explain, 'This is to represent the light of Jesus. Jesus is present with us now.'
- Read the Bible passage chosen for the evening, or tell it as a story (see the section on how to read Scripture with people with learning disabilities, pp. 24–7).

Allow a time of silence for the word to sink in.

- Now give some time for discussion on the theme of the reading. This could either be with the whole group, or in small groups, or in two groups: family members in one group, and friends and people with learning disabilities in another group. This can allow each group to discuss at an appropriate level. Ask each to make a link between the reading and their own daily life. Parents can appreciate times of mutual peer sharing and support on their own.
- Invite each group to bring to the prayer one or two words, or a symbol which summarizes their sharing. The symbol could be made, drawn or chosen from a selection of images or objects.
- Invite people to participate in the suggested activities for the evening. This could again be as one whole group, or two groups: family members in one group, and friends and people with learning disabilities in another group. This can allow family members to continue discussing, and others to do something more action based.
- Have a time of prayer *(see the 12 outline celebrations)* and end with the Lord's Prayer and a familiar song.

CELEBRATION

- Sing *Happy Birthday* to anyone with a birthday in the past month.
- Give news of upcoming events and invite each to add their own important events.
- End with a meal or simply tea and biscuits.
- Invite each person to help with the clearing up – we are all in it together!

Note: In the first session, propose some ground rules to be agreed by all, for example:

- Limit prayers out loud to one thing only, in order to allow time for others to pray.
- Listen when others are speaking.

FAREWELL

- This is a time to remind people of the next gathering, and of anything they might need to prepare for it, or to bring to it.
- People like to take something home. It can be good to give something small as a symbol of the theme of that week, e.g. a paper bird, a paper boat, an image, a badge that has been made, a piece of fruit.
- A group may develop their own ritual of farewell, e.g. holding hands in a circle and looking at each one in the group; singing the same farewell song each time.

To summarize: a possible small group celebration outline:

Welcome.
Activity and Prayer:
- Song.
- Explanation of theme.
- Breaking open the word – reading.
- Going deeper into the theme / sharing in pairs, threes or small groups.
- Activities.
- Prayer – responsive action.
- Song.
- Celebration including food and drink.
- Farewell.

There follow 12 outlines for small group celebrations on various themes. You will notice one celebration is based on the story of the Visitation, which you will also find in the sample church services. This gives an idea of how the same reading can be used very differently.

N.B. Repetition of songs helps people to learn them. The community begins to develop their own repertoire of well-loved songs. Repetition of activities over the months and years of gathering as a community is also really helpful. St Ignatius sees repetition as a deepening and not just a repeating of the same thing! You do not always have to have an entirely original activity!

1   Building up the body

1 Corinthians 12

Aim

To show how each one is needed to build the body, and love is the greatest gift we can share.

You will need

Props

- A large Bible.
- Flowers, leaves, sticks, twigs or stones to create the outline of a body.
- A rose or another flower, or a bowl of water with essential oil in it.
- An object to pick up, e.g. a book, a ball …
- A heart shape, e.g. a heart-shaped cushion or a large piece of card cut in the shape of a heart and painted red.
- Decorations for the table and for the room, e.g. paper serviettes that could be drawn on, large paper or card cut-outs of people, hearts and flowers. *(See the templates in Appendix 5.)*
- Art materials to paint the cut-outs.
- Food and drinks for a celebration afterwards.

- Bowls and cutting knives.
- Seven fruits, each a colour of the rainbow, e.g.
  Red   apples
  Orange   oranges
  Yellow   bananas
  Green   kiwis
  Blue   blueberries
  Indigo   plums
  Violet   purple grapes

Preparation

Invite people to think of the gift that each person brings to the group.

ACTIVITY AND PRAYER

Welcome songs:

- 'The Hokey Cokey'.
- 'Heads and shoulders, knees and toes'.
- The following popular grace but substituting the name of each person for the word 'food'
  'Thank you God for giving us ......' (name of person) 3 x
  'Right where we are'.
  (After each three people the chorus could be sung)
  'Alleluia praise the Lord', 3 x
  'Right where we are'.

EXPLANATION OF THEME

Leader   Today we are going to think about how we can build up the body by each one giving their own gift, and by all of us growing in love for one another. We are going to make the outline of a body, using flowers, leaves, sticks, twigs and stones.

See the photo on p. 106 for an example of this.

Leader   This means we will have to work together as a group, as one body.

Allow time for the group to create the outline of a body together, using the various materials provided.

| Leader | Let's stand round this body we have made together and admire it. We were all needed to make it. We built the body together. |

BREAKING OPEN THE WORD

| Leader | Now we are going to hear a story from the Bible. The Bible is the book full of stories about God, about Jesus and about the Holy Spirit. In the Bible we read about how much God loves us. Today we are going to hear the words of a man named Paul who said that we are called to be together, like one body. ...... *(Name)* is going to read to us now. |

Read slowly the simplified version of the reading below: one person reads and after each section the leader gives the instructions.

Reading   1 Corinthians 12.12–31; 13.13

| Reader | A body has many parts. All these parts together make up the body. Each part is needed. A foot on its own is no good. |
| Leader | Let's try talking with our feet. |

Allow time for one person or everyone to try this.

Leader	It's impossible isn't it?!
Reader	If all we had were ears, how would we smell anything?
Leader	I'm going to pass round this rose (or another flower, or a bowl of water with essential oil in it). Try to smell the scent with your ears!

Pass round a scented rose, or a bowl of water with essential oil in it.

| Leader | You can't smell with your ears can you?! What are ears for? What do we need to smell something? |

Listen to some answers.

| Reader | So there are many parts of a body – but each has a place and each is needed. The eye cannot say, 'I don't need hands!' |
| Leader | Now, who can pick this object up without using your hands, but just by looking at it? Or try to pick it up with your knees! |

Let some people try this.

| Leader | It's impossible isn't it?! Now try with your hands. |

Let some people try this.

Leader	It works with hands doesn't it? We need our hands.
Reader	When one part of the body suffers, the rest of the body suffers.
Leader	Can anyone say how they feel when they have a headache?

Listen to some answers.

Leader	It's only the head that hurts but the whole of us can feel bad.
Reader	When one part of the body is happy and well, the rest of the body is happy and well.
Leader	When one person laughs, everyone in the room laughs.

Give examples of people in the group who make everyone happy when they are full of joy.

Reader	Now, we all make up the body of Jesus – and we all have different gifts. Some are leaders, some are teachers, some are good at healing, some are good at helping others, some are good at speaking languages, some are good at smiling, some are good at welcoming.
Leader	This is the Word of the Lord.
All	**Amen.**
Leader	Everyone turn and look at the person on your left. That's this direction.

Point to the left. Make sure everyone understands which is the left.

Leader	Now think about the gift that person brings to our group. If you are not sure what to say, the group can help you when it is your turn to speak.

Take time to go round the circle allowing each person time to name the gift of their neighbour on the left.

The leader repeats for each one
...... *(Name)*, you have the gift of ......
Thank you for bringing your special gift to our group. We wouldn't be the same without you. We give thanks for you.

Use the sign that the group knows for 'thank you' and point to the person.

Reader	There are three great gifts: faith, hope and love, but love is the greatest gift.

Place a heart in the centre of the body shape.

Leader	Let's now look at the shape of a person in the centre, and at the heart.

Allow a few moments in silence to look at the image created.

Leader	We each have a gift and we are invited to share our gifts with others.
	The greatest gift that we each have, is love. As St Paul says in the Bible, 'love is the greatest gift.'
	We talk of the church as a body. To build up the body of the church we need to deepen our love for one another. So let's now sing a song about love and how we need to share love with one another. As we sing this song we can pass round the heart, as a sign of us sharing love with each other.
SONG	*'Let there be love shared among us' by Dave Bilbrough.*

PRAYER

Leader	We will now have a time of prayer, sitting together round the body shape in the centre.
SONG	*'One bread, one body, one Lord of all' by John Foley.*
Leader	I invite anyone who would like to, to say a prayer now if they wish. After each prayer we could all sing *'Kumbayah my Lord'*, which means 'Come by here my Lord'. We won't sing the verses, just the chorus.

Or this could be sung after several prayers.

Leader	Let us sit quietly now for a few minutes, with no talking, simply listening to God's voice within us.

Allow a short time of silence, judging how long is appropriate for the group.

Leader	Now let's sing!
SONG	*'The Community Song'* It's me, it's me, it's me who builds *community.*
Leader	To end our prayer time, let's say the Lord's Prayer together as we hold hands around the circle.
	...... *(Name)*, would you like to start the prayer?

CELEBRATION

Divide everyone into four small groups and give each group a task:
- *To set the table beautifully. You can use the cut-out figures of people which you could colour in.*
- *To decorate the room beautifully. You can use the flower shapes which you could colour in.*
- *To prepare a grace to be sung at the start of eating, and a thanksgiving song to sing at the end.*
- *To prepare the food and drinks to be enjoyed.*

Allow time for the groups to do the task they have been given.

Leader   Is every group ready? Yes? Then now we are going to make a rainbow fruit salad together! Find a partner (or a small group of – *number* – people). We will give each pair (or small group) a fruit to cut up and add to the fruit salad bowl. Each fruit is one colour of the rainbow. All the colours are needed to make up the rainbow. Lots of fruits are needed to make a fruit salad.

Give pairs or small groups a different fruit.

Leader   Look, can you see? Lots of different types of fruit are needed for a good fruit salad, and we all worked together to make it.
See how beautifully the table has been set by ...... *(Names).*
And look at how the room and table have been decorated by ...... *(Names).*
Now look at the food and drink that ...... *(Names)* got ready for us.
So now, let ...... *(Names)* lead us in a grace to give thanks for the food, then let's enjoy a time of eating and drinking together. And give thanks for how each person is needed; each person brings a gift to all of us, building the body together!

SONG   *Sing the grace and enjoy the food and drink.*

2   Light in the darkness

John 1.3–5

Aim

To recognize the light of God present in the darkness of our world, and the light of God within each one of us.

You will need

Props

- A large Bible.
- A black cloth lying on the floor in the centre.
- A torch.
- Pictures from newspapers of situations of darkness in the world.
- A large candle in the centre of the cloth.
- Icon / picture of Jesus in the centre, or the Christchild.
- A tea-light and a glass jam jar for each one.
- Long matches and a taper.
- A cupcake and a birthday candle for each person to take away.
- A cupcake for each person to be eaten.

Preparation

Find and cut out pictures from newspapers and magazines of people who are suffering and of places of darkness in the world today.

Decoration

- Lay the black cloth on the floor in the centre and place the large candle – unlit – in the centre of the cloth along with an icon or picture of Jesus, or an image of the Christchild.
- Around the cloth have pictures from newspapers of situations of darkness in the world.

ACTIVITY AND PRAYER

WELCOME

As they arrive, give each person a tea-light in a glass jam jar.

SONG   *'Christ be our light, Shine in our hearts' by Bernadette Farrell.*

EXPLANATION OF THEME

Leader   We live in a world where there are many people who go through difficult times. They live in darkness. But God gives light even when we feel we are in the dark. We are called to share the light of God with people who are going through difficult times, because each of us has the light of God within us.
Look at the pictures around the cloth. What do you see? What do they remind you of? What do you think about or how do you feel when looking at these pictures?
I invite you to talk about an image that catches your attention, then to place it in the centre.

Allow some time for responses.

Leader   We have been speaking about people who feel they live in darkness and about places that are suffering and in the dark.

BREAKING OPEN THE WORD

Leader   We are now going to hear some words from the Bible. The Bible is the book which tells us stories about God, about Jesus and about the Holy Spirit. In the Bible we read of how much God loves us.

Reading   John1.3–5

Leader   God created life, and this life is the light of all people. This light shines in the darkness, and the darkness cannot hide the light.

	This is the Word of the Lord.
All	**Amen.**
Leader	We are now going to close all the curtains and turn off all the lights. This means we will be sitting in the dark. Don't worry. It won't be for long and we are sitting together so we will be quite safe.

If anyone might be frightened by the dark then make sure someone is supporting them, or only dim the lights a little. Have a torch which might be helpful for you as leader to read your notes, or for someone who needs some light.

Leader	Now let's sit together in silence in the darkness for a time. People might like to name – either aloud or in their hearts – people they know who are going through a dark time, maybe feeling hopeless, sad and depressed.

Allow time for this.

Leader	Who would like to light the candle in the centre?

Choose someone to do this.

Leader	Thank you …… *(Name)*. See what a difference just a little light can make in the darkness of the whole room. As we heard in the Bible reading: God's light shines in the darkness, and the darkness cannot hide the light.
	Let's take a few moments now to share with a neighbour about how it was for you in the dark. How did you feel? Then share how you felt once the candle was lit.

Allow time for this.

Leader	Now let's reflect on how we can bring light into dark places.

Allow time for this. The leader could help by giving some examples to set people off, e.g. pray for someone, send a card to a prisoner of conscience, give some money to a homeless charity, listen and talk to someone who is sad or lonely, visit someone who lives alone, make a cake for a refugee …

Leader	Listen now to some more words from the Bible.
Reader	Matthew 5.14–16: Jesus said to the people listening to him, 'You are the light of the world … No one lights a lamp and then hides it under a basket, but puts it on a lampstand, so that it can give light to all in the house. In the same way, let your light shine before others, so that they may see the good works you do, and give thanks to God in heaven.
Leader	This is the Word of the Lord.
All	**Amen.**

Leader   Every time we help someone else who is going through a difficult, dark time, we are being light in their darkness, we are being a part of the light of the world.

You might now like to name – either aloud or in your hearts – the sources of light or the people of light in the situations of darkness you have named.

Allow time for this. The leader could model by giving some examples to set people off, e.g. 'I give thanks for nurses in hospital …/ for (name) who visits his elderly grandmother every week' …

Leader   After each prayer let's all say 'Amen'.

Allow time for this.

Leader   When we lit the candle in the darkness, it was no longer dark. We could see because of the light. Let us listen again to the words of Jesus from the Bible:

Reader   John 8.12: Jesus said to his friends, 'I am the light of the world. Whoever follows me will never walk in darkness but will have the light of life.'

Leader   This is the Word of the Lord.

All   **Amen.**

Leader   We need the light of Jesus so we can walk in the light, helping each other and loving each other.

PRAYER

Leader   I invite each one of you to light the tea-light in your jam jar from the candle in the centre using a long taper. Then place it on the cloth in the centre where there is an image of darkness; it might be the one you spoke about earlier. As you do this you could say a prayer out loud if you wish, or silently in your heart.

After each prayer let's all say 'Amen'.

Allow time for this.

Leader   Let us sit quietly now for a few minutes, with no talking, simply listening to God's voice within us, as we look at the cloth and the lights in front of us. See, now there are lots of lights, how the room is much brighter and there is very little darkness.

Allow a short time of silence, judging how long is appropriate for the group.

Leader   To end our prayer time, let's say the Lord's Prayer together as we hold hands around the circle.

…… *(Name)*, would you like to start the prayer?

SONG   'Shine, Jesus, shine' by Graham Kendrick.

CELEBRATION

SONG   'This little light of mine' by Bob Gibson.

Leader   I invite each of you to put a birthday candle on a cupcake. There is one for each person here. Then take them home to give to someone you know who is in need of some light and joy in their life. Don't light the candle until you give it to the person!

Allow time for this.

Share the food and drink that has been brought and prepared – and enjoy! And ensure there are cupcakes to eat there and then, as well as the cupcakes to be taken away in case some people find it too difficult not to be allowed to eat theirs!

3 Encouragement

The Visitation   Luke 1.39–56

Aim

To help people see how we need each other: each person needs the other, and each person can help the other.

You will need

Props

- A large Bible.
- A large copy of the painting of *The Visitation* by Claudia Williams.
- A pastry bowl.
- A wooden spoon.
- A jug of milk.
- A bowl of eggs.
- A key.
- A headscarf for Mary.
- An apron for Elizabeth.
- A copy of the drawing of the two people giving and receiving *(see p. 121)*.
- Pictures of powerless, hungry, poor people from around the world and locally if possible.

Preparation

- Prepare pancakes which could be tossed, or if possible, make them during the celebration.
- Find a version of the Magnificat to sing that people enjoy or could learn.

WELCOME

ACTIVITY AND PRAYER

SONG   *A cheerful 'Welcome' song with actions.*

EXPLANATION OF THEME

Leader   Today we are going to look at the story of the Visitation, a story
                from the Bible. The Bible is the book which tells us stories about
                God, about Jesus and about the Holy Spirit. In the Bible we read of
                how much God loves us. Today's story is about Mary, the mother
                of Jesus, and her cousin, Elizabeth. Mary was expecting the baby
                Jesus. She felt alone and needed someone to talk to who would
                understand her and what she was living through. She needed
                encouragement. So she went to see Elizabeth.
                In the same way, we need each other. It is hard to be alone.
                Elizabeth affirmed Mary. She gave Mary her support. She recog-
                nized that Mary was expecting a baby who was the son of God.
                In the same way, we can affirm each other. We can support each
                other. We can give the other person what they need. We can
                recognize the presence of God in the other person.
                Mary and Elizabeth were full of joy together. They rejoiced. Then
                Mary burst into song, a song about how God lifts up people who
                feel down and no good, a song about how God is faithful forever.

Sing a version of the Magnificat the group know and enjoy.

BREAKING OPEN THE WORD

Reading   Luke 1.39–56

Leader   An angel, a messenger of God, appeared to Mary and told her
                she was going to have a baby and that the baby's father would be
                God himself. Then the angel left Mary. Once she knew she was
                expecting a baby, and that the baby's father was God himself, she
                felt very alone. So she went to visit her cousin Elizabeth who lived
                in a village in the hills. Elizabeth was also expecting a baby, which
                was a miracle as she was too old to have babies.
                As soon as Mary arrived at Elizabeth's home, Elizabeth was filled
                with joy and with the Holy Spirit. She cried out, 'You are the most
                happy of all women! Blessed is the baby you carry within you. As
                soon as I heard your voice my own baby jumped for joy inside me!

Blessed are you because you believed God would keep his promise to you.'
Then Mary too was full of joy and sang a song praising God.
After three months Mary returned to her own home.
This is the Word of the Lord.

All   **Amen.**

Leader   We are now going to act out this story. Look first at this painting of the Visitation. What do you see in it?

Allow time for responses. Point out the modern dress and modern home.

Leader   Mary gave birth to Jesus two thousand years ago but we are asked to give birth to Jesus today, in our own lives, a bit like in this modern painting where we see a young woman pregnant with God.
                Let's set up a table as in the painting, with a jug, bowl, wooden spoon, eggs, a key, a towel …

Set the scene as in the painting.

Leader   Who would like to be Mary and who would like to be Elizabeth?

Choose the actors. It is good to choose one person with, and one without, learning disabilities. If 'Elizabeth' is a person with learning disabilities, she could have a 'servant' to help her do the actions. Similarly, if 'Mary' is a person with learning disabilities, she could have a 'servant' to support her.

Leader   Elizabeth was cooking. She was beating eggs in a bowl. Then she added milk from a jug into the mixture. She was expecting a baby but she was too old to have children unless God made it possible.

Elizabeth acts beating eggs and adding milk.

Leader   Mary arrived. She stood in the doorway and looked shy and unsure.

Mary knocks and opens a door, or mimes this.

Leader   Mary said, 'Elizabeth – you really are going to have a baby! The angel told me you were even though you are so old, and now I see it for myself. It's true!'

Mary looks joyfully at Elizabeth.

Leader   Mary was welcomed with great joy by Elizabeth.

The two women come together and hug each other. The person who does not have a learning disability may have to take the lead in this.

Leader   Elizabeth said, 'And I see you are going to have a baby too!'
                Now, could Mary and Elizabeth stay together in the centre and freeze in position for a few moments as we look at how they

welcome each other with joy? I wonder how Elizabeth and Mary felt about having a baby? What do you think?

Allow some time for responses as Elizabeth and Mary continue to embrace and look happy.

Leader   Elizabeth and Mary, you can move now! We are going to continue the story.

Elizabeth and Mary were so pleased to see each other. How is it for you when you see someone you love after a long time? Or when you feel the need of their friendship? How do you show your love?

Allow some time for responses.

Leader   Elizabeth then said to Mary, 'Happy are you among all women! Happy is your baby who will soon be born!

Why should this great thing happen to me, that the mother of my God comes to visit me?

For as soon as I heard your voice my baby jumped with joy inside me!

Happy are you because you believed God's promise to you!'

Elizabeth, can you stand back and look at Mary and look really happy?

I wonder how you feel when you share good news with a friend, or you hear good news from a friend?

Allow some time for responses.

Leader   Then Mary sang with joy. We are now going to listen to, or to sing if you know the song, that song of Mary. Mary – feel free to dance as we sing! Maybe other people would like to join in with the dancing?

SONG   *The Magnificat by Brian Halferty, or another version known by the group.*

Leader   How do you celebrate good news?

Allow some time for responses.

Leader   Thank you Mary and Elizabeth! Well done! You can rest now.

Mary sang her joy and as she did, she thought of other people in need. When we rejoice do we think of other people? Or do we think only of ourselves and the good thing that has happened to us? Take some time with a friend and share about this now.

Allow time for reflection. Would anyone like to say anything?
Allow time for some responses.

Leader   The story of the Visitation tells us just how much Elizabeth and Mary needed each other. Now let's look at this picture:

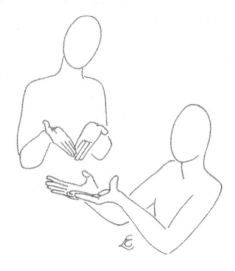

Leader   Elizabeth helped Mary by affirming her and welcoming her.
Mary helped Elizabeth by being there to support her during her pregnancy. It can't have been easy for an old woman to expect a baby.
Each needed help from the other. Each gave help to the other.

Take some time now to reflect on the following two questions as you look at the drawing above:

Leader   Who is giving? Who is receiving?
How do we give and take in our family, or in our home, or in our church or community?
Take some time now with a friend to think about these two questions.

Allow time for reflection.

Leader   Would anyone like to say anything in the big group?

Allow time for some responses.

Leader   In your pairs, choose who will be A and who will be B. If you can't choose, then the person with the longest hair can be A!
Can all the As stand, and all the Bs sit on a chair in front of their partner?

Allow time for this.

Leader   Now can all the Bs stand, and all the As sit on a chair in front of their partner?

Take some time now to discuss:
- How you felt standing/sitting?
- In which position did you feel strong? Weak? Comfortable? Uncomfortable?
- Which position did you prefer?

Try the same, but holding your hands as in the drawing. Swap round so each of you has a chance to stand, and to sit:
- Who is giving? Who is receiving?
- How can we give and receive?
- Discuss this with your partner.

Allow time for this.

PRAYER

Place the painting of The Visitation in the centre.

SONG   *A version of the 'Magnificat'. It could be good to repeat the one already used.*

Repeat the reading from above.

Leader   In her song the 'Magnificat', Mary spoke of people who are poor and in difficult situations. She says God will help them, he will raise them up. I invite you now to choose a picture from the pile at the side. They are pictures of people who are poor and suffering, like the ones Mary sang about. In your own time, you could place the picture you choose in the centre and say a prayer at the same time if you wish. If not, we can just pray in silence for people such as these, the homeless, refugees, prisoners ... After each prayer let's all say 'Amen'.
              Let us sit quietly now for a few minutes, with no talking, simply listening to God's voice within us.

Allow a short time of silence, judging how long is appropriate for the group.

Leader   To end our prayer time, let's say the Lord's Prayer together as we hold hands around the circle. ...... *(Name)* would you like to start the prayer?

FINAL SONG *Another version of the 'Magnificat'.*
              OR 'The Lord hears the cry of the poor' by John B. Foley.

CELEBRATION

Make and toss pancakes or make Scotch pancakes. Sit round the table set up like the painting with its bowl of eggs and jug of milk and simply enjoy the pancakes together.

4   Welcome

Aim

To help people understand the gift of welcome, and to understand that God invites us all into the heart of the dance of love in the Trinity; to see that God keeps his promises.

You will need

Props

- A large Bible.
- Small copies of the Icon of the Trinity hanging from a tree (made of branches in a pot) – one per person.
- Abraham – a brown cloak.
- Sarah – a shawl.
- Angels – white cloths or white cassocks.
- Bread.
- Grapes.
- A bowl.

- A jug of water.
- A towel.
- A cloth to hang to make a tent with an opening.
- Some pot plants to be the oak trees.
- A baby doll (a live baby would be great!).
- Easy-peel oranges and paper serviettes.
- Special tablecloths to decorate the tables for the celebration at the end.
- A dictionary of names and their meanings, or an easily accessible website for this.

Preparation

- Invite some new people to the group and find a way to give them a special welcome.
- Choose people to be Abraham, Sarah, the servant, and the three angels.
- Look up the meaning of each group member's name in advance.

WELCOME

Especially of any new people.

SONG   *'Come all you people, come and praise your maker' (x 3).*
                'Come now and worship the Lord' (Uyai mose tinnemate mwari
                (x 3), uyai mose zvino) by Alexander Gondo.

ACTIVITY AND PRAYER

EXPLANATION OF THEME

Leader   We are encouraged to welcome other people, but God wants to
                welcome us all into the heart of the Trinity. God keeps his promises
                and brings us joy.

Project the image of the Trinity or show a large icon of the Trinity

Leader   Today we are going to be looking at a story in the Bible about a
                man called Abraham. The Bible is the book which tells us stories
                about God, about Jesus and about the Holy Spirit. In the Bible we
                read of how much God loves us. Today's story is about Abraham
                welcoming three strangers. These three strangers can be seen as the
                Trinity: the Father, Jesus and the Holy Spirit. Look now at the icon
                of the Trinity.

*Point out the three persons of the Trinity, the table with the food, and the empty
space where we are invited to enter into the heart of God.*

BREAKING OPEN THE WORD

Reading   Genesis 18.1–15

Leader	We are going to hear the story from the Bible now. Let's try to act out the story as we hear it. Who would like to be Abraham? The three strangers? Sarah? The servant?

Choose some people.

Leader	Thank you! Let's now hang this cloth by the pot plants which can be the oak trees, to make a tent. And we'll place the bread, grapes, bowl, jug of water and towel ready inside the tent. Are we all ready? Then let's begin.

Abraham was sitting at the entrance to his tent at the hottest time of the day. His tent was in the shade of some oak trees. He saw three strangers coming up to him. He stood up and ran to welcome them. He asked them to stay. He offered to wash their feet with water, and to let them stay a while and rest in the shade of the trees. He offered to give them bread to eat.

Abraham sits at the entrance to the tent. Three strangers come up to him. He gestures to them that they are welcome.

Leader	The strangers were happy to be welcomed and agreed to stay for a while. As they sat and rested, Abraham asked his wife Sarah to make cakes, while he chose a young calf and gave it to a servant to cook. He gave the guests the food when it was ready and stood watching as they ate.

The three strangers sit. Abraham gestures to Sarah and the servant to prepare food and then washes the feet of the three strangers. The servant gives them bread and grapes to eat.

Leader	The strangers said, 'Where is your wife, Sarah?' Abraham said, 'There, in the tent.'

Abraham points to the tent. Sarah peeks out from behind the cloth listening.

Leader	The strangers said, 'When we return, your wife Sarah will have a baby boy.' Sarah was listening from inside the tent and laughed. She and Abraham were too old to have children so she could not believe the strangers.

Sarah laughs.

Leader	The strangers said, 'Why did Sarah laugh? Doesn't she believe that God can work wonderful miracles? When we return, Sarah shall indeed have a son.' Sarah said, 'I didn't laugh!' Sarah was afraid and that's why she laughed.
Strangers	'Oh yes, you did laugh.'
Leader	After some months, Sarah did indeed give birth to a baby boy, even though she was too old to have children. Abraham gave the boy the name 'Isaac' which means 'Laughter'. Sarah said, 'God gave me laughter! Everyone who hears this story will laugh with joy with me.'

Sarah enters with Abraham and a baby, a very young child or a baby doll. They dance with joy. Play joyful dance music for this.

Leader	This is the Word of the Lord.
All	**Thanks be to God.**
Leader	Have a look at the icon. What do you see?

Listen to responses from the group.

Leader	*Pointing to the relevant parts of the icon:* There are three people, the three strangers that Abraham welcomed. There is a table and the meal he prepared for them. The three people could also be the Father, Jesus and the Holy Spirit. They form a circle. There is a space where we who are looking at the picture can be invited in to join the feast at the table with the Father, Jesus and the Holy Spirit. I invite you now to get into small groups.

If necessary help to facilitate this.

Leader	In your small group share memories of special meals you remember and the importance of mealtimes.

Allow time for this.

Leader	Would anyone like to share anything you said in your small group now in the larger group?

Allow time for this.

Leader	I have here some easy-peel oranges, one for each person. Turn to a partner, and if there is an uneven number then I can join in to make a pair. I invite you to share your orange with your partner. When one has shared, then allow the other person to share their orange with you.

Allow time for this.

| Leader | Has everyone finished? Now take a few moments to say how it was to share food with another, and how it was to be given food. |

Allow time for this.

PRAYER

Project the image of the icon of the Trinity or place an icon of the Trinity as a focal point for prayer.

| Leader | I invite you all now to look at the icon again and imagine yourself being invited into the centre of the circle of love of the Trinity. |

| SONG | *'Come to the circle' by John Coleman – include the names of people present, e.g. 'Welcome to the circle (Name ...... and Name ......)'.* |

| Leader | Sarah gave her child the name 'Isaac' which means 'Laughter'. Many names have special meanings. How does your name call you to be a daughter or son of God? It can be good to try to be faithful to the name we have been given, e.g. Isabelle means 'given to God'. Let's look at the meaning of each of our names now. |

Give the meaning of each person's name in turn. Try to find a way of explaining the name meaningfully, e.g. George means a farmer or earthworker, i.e. someone who is grounded and humble, hard working and a provider of food.

Affirm each person in the gift of their name, e.g.

| Leader | George, thank you for the hard worker you are. May you always be grounded and humble. May you always nourish others through your words and actions.
I invite anyone who would like to, to say a prayer now if they wish. After each prayer let's all say 'Amen'.
Let us sit quietly now for a few minutes, with no talking, simply listening to God's voice within us. |

Allow a short time of silence, judging how long is appropriate for the group.

| Leader | To end our prayer time, let's say the Lord's Prayer together as we hold hands around the circle. ......(Name), would you like to start the prayer? |

FINAL SONG

> *'Hamba nathi kululu wethu'*
> *'Come with me for the journey is long …'*
> *South African traditional (tr. © Lutheran World Federation)*
>
> *Add your own verses, e.g.*
> *Eat with me for the journey is long …*
> *Pray with me for the journey is long …*
> *Laugh with me for the journey is long …*

CELEBRATION

Have a bring and share meal.
Decorate the table beautifully to welcome new people in a special way.

Divide into two groups:
- *one group prepare the savoury part of the meal and serve it to the others.*
- *the other group prepare the sweets and drinks and serve it to the others.*

Leader   I invite each one to take an icon from the tree as they leave. The icon shows the story we thought about today and is a reminder of how God invites us into the heart of the Trinity.

5   Searching and finding

Aim

To reflect on the treasure of simple daily life at home.

You will need

Props

- A large Bible.
- Gold chocolate coins – enough for at least one for everyone.
- A 'treasure chest' (this could be a large box covered with gold paper).
- Ten large gold coins made out of card. Put nine in the treasure chest and keep one apart.
- A broom.
- Cloths or shawls (simple costumes) for the housewife and other women.
- The music for the Israeli wedding blessing dance 'Nigun Atik' and a means of playing it (this can be found on YouTube).

Preparation

- Prepare photos to be projected of the various parts of a home: an open front door, a kitchen, a meal, people doing the dishes, a prayer corner, a sitting room, a bedroom, a bathroom.

- Choose someone who could keep the tenth silver coin hidden and be trusted to show it at the right time when the gospel story is acted out.
- Select a second person to be the servant of the woman who lost her coin. Explain what the servant needs to do in the drama: to hand the treasure chest to the woman, then to help her open the chest and count out the coins, one at a time; then to give her a broom.

WELCOME

SONG   *Any joyful songs with actions the group enjoys.*

EXPLANATION OF THEME

Leader   Today we are going to think about a story from the Bible, the book which tells us stories about God, about Jesus and about the Holy Spirit. In the Bible we read of how much God loves us. This story is about a woman who lost a coin, and celebrated when she found it again. The woman is like God, and we are like the lost coin. If we turn away from God, God will do all she can to find us again, and then when we turn back to God, she will celebrate with us because God loves each one of us and will do all she can to make us love her. Did you notice I called God 'she'? God is like our father but God is also like our mother. Let's listen to the story now.

BREAKING OPEN THE WORD

Reading   Luke 15.8–10

Reader   There was once a woman who had ten silver coins. Then one day she lost one of them. She was really upset that she had lost the coin. It was very valuable and she needed it. She lit a lamp, took a broom and then swept her whole house. She searched carefully in every corner of her house until she found it. When she finally found it, she called together her friends and neighbours, saying, 'Come and celebrate with me, for I have found my coin which was lost.'

                 Jesus said, 'Just like the joy of that woman finding her lost coin, the angels of God rejoice with joy over each person who has turned away from God but then returns to God.'

Leader   This is the Word of the Lord.

All   **Thanks be to God.**

Leader	We are now going to act this story out. We need the woman who lost the coin. Who wants to play this part?

Choose someone to play this part.

Leader	There was once a woman who had ten gold coins.

Gesture to the woman to come forward in front of everyone and to the servant to bring her the treasure chest.

Leader	One day she counted out her coins. One – Two – Three – Four – Five –Six –Seven – Eight – Nine …

Pause after each number so everyone can repeat the number after you.
The 'servant' helps the 'woman' take out one coin at a time and hold it high so all can see it as the leader counts.

Leader	A coin was missing! She only had nine coins, not ten! Where was the tenth coin?! She had lost it! She was really upset that she had lost the coin. It was very valuable and she needed it.

Gesture to the woman to look upset!

Leader	So the woman took a broom and swept her whole house, searching carefully in every corner of her house.

The servant should hand the woman a broom and support her to sweep everywhere, making everyone watching stand up so she can sweep where they had been sitting, under their chairs and everywhere.

Leader	She asked everyone to help her search for the coin.

Gesture to everyone to stand up and search for the lost coin.
After some time of searching indicate to the person who has the tenth coin hidden that it is time to stand up and shout out that the coin has been found.

Leader	Finally she found the coin! She was so happy! She counted out all her coins once more to check she really had all ten.

The servant should bring the treasure chest to the woman and help her count out the coins once more.

Leader	One – Two – Three – Four – Five –Six –Seven – Eight – Nine … TEN! The woman was so full of joy that she then called together her friends and neighbours, saying, 'Come and celebrate with me, for I have found my coin which was lost.'
SONG	*A song of rejoicing.*

| Leader | Jesus said, 'Just like the joy of that woman finding her lost coin, God in heaven celebrates over each person who has turned away from God but then returns to God.' So let's celebrate together now by learning a dance. |

Teach the Israeli wedding blessing dance or some other simple dance that all can join in.

| Leader | Can you now get into small groups of three? Ask each other what is your treasure in your home, and what is holy in your homes? Treasure is something that is really important to you. Holy means something that is set aside for God. |

Allow time for the groups to share.

| Leader | Would anyone like to say something of what you shared to the whole group? |

Allow time for some responses.

| Leader | We are now going to look at some photos of homes, e.g.:
- An open front door – *welcome.*
- A kitchen – *cooking together, creating a good meal, chatting.*
- A meal – *fun and celebration at meals, good food.*
- People doing the dishes – *therefore taking time together and chatting.*
- A prayer corner – *time to quietly offer the day to God and give thanks, to pray for one another and our world.*
- A sitting room – *Jean Vanier says 'To love someone is to waste time with them.' Space to relax and enjoy being together.*
- A bedroom – *the importance of our own intimate space.*
- A bathroom – *helping another/caring for myself: St Paul wrote, 'Do you not know that your body is the temple of the Holy Spirit?'* |

As the photos are shown invite people to speak of the holy treasure they discover in daily life at home and wasting time together. Some suggestions are above.

PRAYER

| Leader | I invite anyone who would like to, to say a prayer now if they wish. After each prayer let's all say 'Amen'.
Let us sit quietly now for a few minutes, with no talking, simply listening to God's voice within us. |

Allow a short time of silence, judging how long is appropriate for the group.

Leader   To end our prayer time, let's say the Lord's Prayer together as we hold hands around the circle. Name …, would you like to start the prayer?

FINAL SONG *'I have the joy, joy, joy, joy down in my heart' by George W. Cooke.*

Leader   I invite you now when you go home to reflect on the treasure you can find there.

CELEBRATION

Give each person some gold chocolate coins and invite them to share their treasure (the gold coins) with others at home or with their neighbours.

CLOSING SONG

A joyful action song or 'Give thanks with a grateful heart'.

6 Forgiveness and Reconciliation

Aim

To help people understand the importance of doing all they can to build the sense of community and unity; to ask forgiveness for the times we break the unity of love in a group.

Summer is a good time for this celebration. Part of the celebration could be outside in a garden. If it is indoors then you will need to adapt the latter part of the celebration.

You will need

Props

- A bundle of sticks tied with a gold or white ribbon.
- Soil and compost.
- A rake.
- A small tree to be planted.
- Heart-shaped cards or pieces of paper *(see Appendix 5)*.
- Pens.

Preparation

Make heart-shaped biscuits filled with jam.

WELCOME

ACTIVITY AND PRAYER

SONG   *A joyful action song of welcome.*

EXPLANATION OF THEME

Leader   Today we are going to hear a story, a story about a bundle of sticks! It is a story about the importance of doing all we can to build our community or group together, and of staying united. Of course there are times we can hurt each other, but if we forgive each other we can keep the unity in the group.

BREAKING OPEN THE WORD

Reading   A story from the oral tradition.

Leader   There was once a father who had five sons who were constantly quarrelling. One day, tired by their quarrelling, the father asked his sons to bring him a bundle of sticks. Handing the bundle to the oldest son he told him to break the bundle. The young man tried to break the sticks over his knee, but all he got was a sore leg. One by one the other brothers were given the same command. None of them were able to break the bundle.

Pass round the bundle of sticks and invite people to break the bundle in two.

Leader   See, no one managed to break the bundle of sticks on their own! But some of you tried very, very hard!
Finally, the father tore open the bundle and handed each son a single stick.
'Break this,' he said. They all easily managed to break the single stick.
The father said to his sons, 'If you stay together and help one another you will have the strength of this bundle of sticks. No one will be able to break you. But if you are divided among yourselves you will be broken as easily as these sticks which you broke.'

Untie the bundle and give each person one stick.

Leader Now as you hold your stick, take some time to think of something you have done that hurt someone else.

Allow time for this.

Leader In your own time, think about what you did. If you feel sorry that you hurt someone else, then break the stick in two. We will do this in silence.

Allow time for this.

Leader We can hurt another person and then our friendship can be broken like our sticks were broken just now. We are no longer together, but are separate.

Now I invite you to make a cross with your two pieces of stick. A partner could help you if needed. You just need to hold the two pieces of stick together in the form of a cross. You don't need to tie them together.

Allow time for this.

Leader Now look at your cross. Do you remember the stories in the Bible about how Jesus loved everyone, even those who hurt him? Do you remember how he died on a cross, killed by people who hated him? Do you remember that when he was dying on the cross he said, 'Forgive them because they don't know what they are doing'? He forgave the people who were putting him to death! Jesus is always ready to forgive us when we are sorry for hurting someone else.

TWO ALTERNATIVE WAYS TO CONTINUE:

1 FOR INSIDE

Leader Jesus calls us back into community. He calls us to forgive each other. He wants us to be together as one body. So I invite you now to undo the cross and then together use your two pieces of stick to form the outline of a body on the floor in the centre of the room, on top of the cloth that is lying there. We have done this at an earlier celebration which you might remember. (Building up the Body, p. 106.)

Allow time for this.

Leader Now let's stand round the body and hold hands if we can. We are together. Together we form one body, one community, one group.

Look round the circle at each person and silently give thanks for the gift of each person.

* For the rest of the prayer see the asterisk below.

2 FOR OUTSIDE

Leader   Let us now go out into the garden.

Lead everyone to a place already chosen where a fire can be lit.

Leader   We are now going to burn our sticks.

Allow time for this.

Leader   Let's stand together round the fire holding hands. The sticks are the symbol of the different ways we have hurt each other. But now they are being burnt. God burns away our mistakes in the fire of his love and calls us together. He forgives us and loves us and wants us to be together. He wants us to love one another. We are together when we love one another and forgive each other.

Take time to burn the sticks. Make sure everyone is safe!

PRAYER

Have a candle in a glass jar so it won't be blown out by the breeze, and flowers in a vase.

SONG   *'Bind us together Lord' by Bob Gillman.*

Reading   Psalm 133

It is good to live together as brothers and sisters. It is like precious oil flowing down over the whole body, it is like the dew falling in the morning on a mountain top. God blesses people who live peacefully together. He gives them life which never ends.

Leader   See the hole in the ground here? Let's put the ash from our sticks in the hole.

Allow time to do this.

Leader   We are now going to plant a tree in the hole. The ashes from our burnt sticks will help the tree to grow well. In the same way God can bring good out of even painful situations.

PLANT A TREE

Symbolizing the tree of life and God's love.

Each person places a handful of soil in the hole where the tree has been planted and then waters the tree.
Play music during this.

* From this point the prayer is the same whether inside or outside.

Leader	I invite anyone who would like to, to say a prayer if they wish now. After each prayer let's all say 'Amen'.
	Let us sit quietly now for a few minutes, with no talking, simply listening to God's voice within us.

Allow a short time of silence, judging how long is appropriate for the group.

Leader	John 15.15, 17 'I call you friends … Love one another.'
SONG	*'Jubilate Deo', Taizé chant.*
Leader	We are now going to give to each person a heart-shaped card. Draw or write on it as you wish. You may want to draw the person you've hurt. You may want to write a word that you would like to say to the person or to God.
	In your own time, place your heart round the plant or tree *(or in the centre of the body if you stayed inside)* and if you wish, you can say a prayer out loud for the person you've hurt.
	To end our prayer time, let's say the Lord's Prayer together as we hold hands around the circle. …… *(Name)*, would you like to start the prayer?

FINAL SONG *'Let there be love shared among us' by Dave Bilbrough.*

CELEBRATION

Eat pre-prepared heart-shaped biscuits filled with jam (or biscuits cut in the shape of hearts). Before and after eating, sing some joyful action songs.

7 Discovering the Most Important Thing

Aim

To help people recognize beauty and treasure even in the small things of everyday life, and in each other; to help people see we can only receive more by letting go of what we have.

You will need

Props

- A large Bible.
- A transparent glass bowl of water.
- Lots of 'pearls' (coloured glass stones of different shapes, sizes and colours).
- A basket for the glass stones.
- Paper and pens – enough for each person.

Preparation

- Two people primed to share the 'pearls of value' they have discovered in the littleness of everyday life.

- Two people primed to share a few moments when the sharing of pearls – acts of loving kindness – have helped to transform themselves or others. They should be asked to bring a picture or object to illustrate or symbolize what they say.
- Ensure people bring food to share for the celebration at the end.

ACTIVITY AND PRAYER

SONG   *Favourite 'Welcome' action songs.*

Leader   Let's move the chairs into a circle so we can all see each other.

SONG   *'We hold a treasure not made of gold' by John B. Foley.*

BREAKING OPEN THE WORD

Leader   Let's begin by listening to a short story from the Bible. The Bible is the book which tells us stories about God, about Jesus and about the Holy Spirit. In the Bible we read of how much God loves us:

Reading   Matthew 13.45–46

The Kingdom of heaven is like a person who was looking for beautiful expensive pearls. When he found one of great value, he went and sold everything he owned and bought the pearl.
This is the Word of the Lord.

All   **Amen.**

EXPLANATION OF THEME

Leader   There are three parts to this short story:
First a person is SEARCHING.
Then the person RECOGNIZES what is of great value, what is most important in life.
Finally the person has the CONFIDENCE and BELIEF to sell all they own in order to have what is most important in life.
We live in a world filled with precious pearls. Pearls are precious stones. They are worth a LOT of money. If you sold one you could buy many things with the money you got from selling it. We talk about 'pearls of beauty', 'pearls of wisdom', 'pearls of truth'.
In some ways, we are all like the person who was looking for the pearl of great value. We are looking for the pearl of beauty, or the pearl of meaning or the pearl of wisdom. Like the person in the story, we are SEARCHING for what will give us life and happiness.

The trouble is, we are not always very good at recognizing pearls of great value when we see them. We do not always recognize what is beautiful, what is wise, what is true. We need to have eyes and hearts that are open so we can RECOGNIZE the true treasure which will give us life and happiness, like the person who recognized the value of the pearl they found.

SEARCHING

Leader   Imagine you are a jewellery shop owner in search of fine pearls. You see before you a collection of pearls. Some are big and some are small; some are round and some are not; some are one colour and some are multicoloured. Go up and take one that instinctively appeals to you – but please don't take too long choosing. Then go back to your place.

Allow time for people to choose a stone from the bowl of 'pearls' in the centre.

Leader   Now look at your precious pearl. Admire its colour, its shape, its feel. What does it represent for you? Would anyone like to say anything about their 'pearl'?

Allow time for people to speak. It can help to repeat a word that someone says as a way of affirming the person and what they have said.

Leader   Does it remind you of a moment when you've felt something small – but special and significant – was happening? A moment when you had a sense of heaven opening? The poet, William Blake, said: 'to see a world in a grain of sand,/ and a heaven in a wild flower …' What are you searching for in your life today? A place where you feel you belong? Someone you can love – and be loved by? A sense of peace?

Allow a moment of silence for reflection. Some people might then like to say what they are searching for.

Leader   Ask God for what you are still searching for and give thanks in your heart for the gifts you already have, maybe for really small, ordinary things that you haven't realized the beauty of till now.

Allow a moment of silent prayer.

RECOGNIZING

Leader   It can take time to recognize the pearl of beauty in each person, whatever their body looks like. We are too used to believing beauty is only what we see in photos in magazines and in films.

It requires humility to recognize the pearl of meaning in the small, everyday, things of life – especially if we only see God in success and riches. It requires humility to recognize wisdom in the words and actions of people with little or no education – especially if you think of yourself as well educated and successful.

Two people will now share one or two moments when they've had a sense of discovering a pearl of great value in their life, in very small things that have happened to them. After all, pearls are quite small! For all their smallness, however, these moments are significant in that they seem to speak of times which take us out of ourselves, and help us to see life and ourselves afresh.

Invite the two people you asked to come prepared, to share the 'pearls of value' they have discovered in the littleness of everyday life.

SONG   *'I come like a beggar' by Sydney Carter.*

CONFIDENCE AND BELIEF

Leader   Before the person who had found the pearl of great value could buy it, they first had to sell all that they had. Often, if we really want to treasure the value of something, we have to give up something else. There is a story about a monkey who saw a banana in a trap with an opening slightly bigger than the monkey's hand. The monkey put its paw into the trap and grabbed the food so its paw turned into a fist – too big to get back through the opening. The monkey was so determined to keep the food it would not let go, and so was stuck. No matter how hard it tried, its paw could not be freed from the trap.

The only way the monkey could free its paw was to let go of the food.

Now I invite you to hold your pearl tightly in your hand.

Check that all understand what to do or have some support to do this.

I'm now going to try to pour more pearls into your hand.

Go to each person and try to pour some of the stones into their closed hands.

It doesn't work when your hand is closed does it?
Now let's try with your hand open.

Go to each person again and try the same thing.

> This time you can receive more can't you?!
>
> We all like being in control – of ourselves, of others and of God. But Jean Vanier, the founder of L'Arche, says that the path of holiness is in moving from closedness to openness: allowing ourselves to open up and to hear God speaking to us.
>
> Try making a fist again – use both hands. How do your hands feel?

Listen to some responses – repeat key words. People may say words like 'tired', 'tight', 'closed up' …

Leader   Now let your fist go. Feel the difference. How do your hands feel now?

Listen to some responses – repeat key words. People may say words like 'relief', 'openness' …

Leader   This is like the story of the person who sold everything they had so they could have the pearl they wanted. They let go everything and then received the thing of greatest value.

What makes us close up? What makes us hold on to things we should let go of? We are going to think about this now. Could everyone put all their pearls into this bowl of water?

Allow time for people to do this.

Leader   Opening up requires that we have trust. And trust is only built up when it is tried and tested. I invite you now to think about your fears.

What makes you fearful or scared?

What do you find difficult to let go of?

What are you trying to hold on to?

Whatever it is – maybe it's a person, a desire or a habit – write or draw this on a piece of paper. Some people may need support to do this. You could work in pairs if that is easier.

Allow time for people to do this. Play some gentle, meditative music during the activity.

Leader   Is everyone ready? Then take turns, and in your own time, put your paper in the water. As you do so, put your hand in deeper and pull out a pearl from the bottom of the bowl. You are letting go of something you have been holding on to, and now you are able to receive something precious, something better and greater. As we do this, we could play some music.

Allow time for people to do this and play some instrumental music during this activity.

SHARING PEARLS

Leader   Does anyone have any ideas about what the person who bought the pearl did after buying it?

Listen to suggestions from the group.

Leader   The truth is, we don't know, as the story stops there. But I think that we can safely say, that having sold everything else in order to possess it, the person treasured the pearl very carefully.

People treasure things in different ways.

Some would jump for joy, as though they've just won the lottery, and would invite friends and relatives round to see it.

Others might look at the pearl and think to themselves: 'It's a great pearl, but to really show it off well I think it should be set in a necklace that everyone can admire.'

Others might just simply make sure it's safe and secure, so it doesn't get stolen or tarnished.

And that's what – more or less – we try to do in our little community here.

We try to treasure one another in a spirit of love, sharing in each other's joys and sorrows. What we do may be only small steps in the eyes of the world – but they are often huge leaps for the person concerned or for each of us. Community is made up of countless little daily acts of loving kindness and forgiveness. They are like the yeast which lifts up our lives. As we use them, they grow more and more. One smile leads to another; one good deed leads to another; joy multiplies.

Two people will now recount a few moments when the sharing of pearls – acts of loving kindness – have helped to transform themselves or others. As each person finishes speaking the picture or object they used will be placed around the bowl of pearls.

Invite some people to talk who have already been given time to prepare. It would help if they had something visual to show, or tactile to touch.

Leader   Look at the pearl you took from the water. It represents one of the ways in which we can transform the lives of others. They are gifts which are not our own, but which are God given – and given for us to share with each other.

PRAYER

Leader   I'd like you to reflect now on what gift God has given you. Maybe it's the gift of telling stories or listening; the gift of being caring or being compassionate; the gift of smiling and bringing joy ... Whatever it is, give thanks to God, and place your pearl in the centre so that together we can make the outline of a heart – the heart representing our community here.

Allow people in turn to place their pearls in the centre and help them to form the shape of a heart with the pearls.

Leader   I invite anyone who would like to, to say a prayer if they wish now. After each prayer let's all say 'Amen'.
                Let us sit quietly now for a few minutes, with no talking, simply listening to God's voice within us.

Allow a short time of silence, judging how long is appropriate for the group.

Leader   To end our prayer time, let's say the Lord's Prayer together as we hold hands around the circle. ...... *(Name)* would you like to start the prayer?

SONG   *'I will sing, I will sing a song unto the Lord' by Max Dyer.*

CELEBRATION

Each brings food they have prepared at home, and share with everyone else.

8   Looking After Each Other

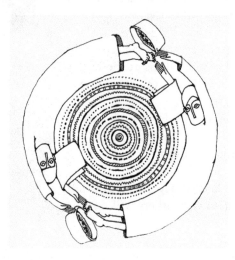

Aim

To obey the command of Jesus to wash each other's feet and through this to discover his 'hidden' beatitude: 'Blessed, happy are you if you do this' – to experience servant leadership and mutuality.

You will need

Props

For every group of eight people:

- A large Bible.
- A bowl.
- A large jug.
- Two white towels (so that once one is too wet, the other can be used).
- A large container of fresh warm(!) water to replenish the jugs when necessary.
- A large container to be filled with dirty water from the bowls as necessary.
- Meditative music to be played quietly during the washing of the feet.

Where possible try to have matching jugs and bowls, and as attractive as possible, i.e. not measuring jugs for example!

Preparation

Choose a leader for each small group and make sure they know what to do. The small group leader models what to do for the rest of the group, i.e.:

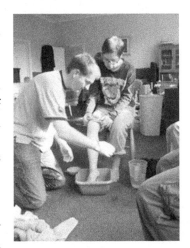

- Takes the bowl from the centre of the group circle, and the jug and towel; kneels at the feet of the person next to her placing the bowl just in front of the person's feet.
- Pours water over one foot of the person, washes it, then dries it.
- Then repeats with the other foot.

This needs to be modelled slowly and prayerfully and with great respect so that others will do it in the same spirit.

Then the small group leader kneels in front of the person whose feet have been washed. This person places their hands on the head or shoulders of the one who has washed their feet, and silently says a prayer for them, then turns to the person next to them and repeats the action. This continues round the circle till the leader's feet are washed. The leader then returns the bowl, jug and towel to the centre.

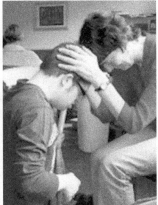

ACTIVITY AND PRAYER

SONG   *'God welcomes all' by John L. Bell.*

EXPLANATION OF THEME

Leader   Today we are going to think about the story of the washing of the
                feet. The washing of the feet took place at the last meal Jesus ate
                with his close friends, the meal where they celebrated the Passover
                together. Today we are going to remember that meal where Jesus
                washed the feet of his friends, teaching them how the leader has to
                be the one who is the servant of the others.

                The Passover celebration was a time when the Jewish people
                looked back at their history, at the good times, and at the difficult
                times. They remembered how God was always there for them and
                helped them through their difficulties. So now, let's look back over
                our last year. What happened in our group over the past year?

Ask some leading questions and encourage responses e.g.

- Who have we welcomed into our group?
- Can anyone remember any difficult moments?
- What funny stories can people remember?
- Do you remember when *(Name)* forgave *(Name)*?
- Who always helped with tea?
- Remember how *(Name)* was sad because his dog died and
  everyone comforted him.
- Remember *(Name)*'s birthday celebration.
- Remember when *(Name)* spoke in the group for the first time.

Leader   What have we learned from one another this year?

Allow time for responses. If necessary give some prompts, e.g.

Leader   How to serve each other, how to make people welcome, how to take
                care of ourselves, and of each other, that we are each welcomed,
                accepted and loved as we are, that to love someone is not to do
                things for them but to waste time with them.

*OR invite someone to talk about what the washing of the feet means to them (this
person would need to be asked in advance so they have time to prepare what they
want to say).*

Show the four photos of the washing of the feet in L'Arche London (see p. 148).

SONG   *'Amen, Siakudumisa!' (Amen, sing praises to the Lord!) by
                C. Molefe.*

BREAKING OPEN THE WORD

Leader   I invite you now to get into small groups of about eight people and to sit in circles.

Alternatively, depending on the size of the group, everyone could sit in one large circle.

Leader   We will begin with a song, then listen to a reading from the Bible, the book which tells us stories about God, about Jesus and about the Holy Spirit. In the Bible we read of how much God loves us. Today's story is about how Jesus washed the feet of his friends. After the reading, we will take time to wash each other's feet.

There is a leader in each group who will start. Then in turn each person does as the leader did. If your group finishes before the others, then just sit quietly in silence until everyone has finished.

If it is one large group, either the leader starts and then will be the last one to have their feet washed, or two people sitting next to each other begin. They then wash the feet of the person on their other side. After the last two have their feet washed, they go to the first people and wash their feet.

SONG   *'Come Holy Spirit, Maranatha' by John L. Bell.*
Or 'Ubi caritas' Taizé chant. (If this Latin chant is sung, then explain it means 'Where Love is, God is'.)

Reading   John 13.1–17

Leader   Jesus knew that he was going to be killed. But he also knew that he came from God and after his death he would return to God. He wanted to have a last meal with his friends, to celebrate with them. He loved them and loved them to the end, yet one of his friends, a man called Judas, was going to betray him and Jesus knew this.
They sat down to eat. In the middle of the meal Jesus got up from the table. He took off his outer cloak, and then tied a towel round his waist. Then he poured water into a basin and began to wash the feet of his friends. Then he dried them with the towel tied round his waist.
Simon Peter was shocked that Jesus, his master and teacher, was going to wash his feet like a servant or slave. He said, 'Lord, are you going to wash my feet?'
Jesus said to him, 'You don't understand what I am doing, but later you will understand.'
Peter said to him, 'You will never wash my feet!'

Jesus answered, 'Unless you let me wash your feet, you can have nothing to do with me.'

Peter then said, 'Then Lord, wash my hands and my head and not just my feet!'

Jesus said, 'When you have had a bath you don't need to wash again, except the feet, for you are completely clean. Peter, you are clean, though not all of you are.' He said this because he knew one of his friends would betray him.

After he had washed their feet and put his cloak back on, he sat down at the table again. Then he said, 'Do you understand what I just did? You call me teacher and Lord, and that is right for I am your teacher and Lord. So if I, your Lord and teacher, have washed your feet, then you must wash each other's feet. I have given you an example, so that you will do as I have done. Servants are not greater than their masters.

If you know this, if you understand what I have just said, and if you wash each other's feet, then you will be blessed, you will be happy.

This is the Word of the Lord.

All   **Thanks be to God.**

THE WASHING OF THE FEET

Play quiet meditative music or Taizé chants during this.
The designated group leader/s start(s) by kneeling at the feet of their neighbour.
When the washing of the feet is done prayerfully in groups of eight it can take up to 20 minutes.
The leader needs to keep an eye to see when everyone has finished. They can help by emptying out dirty water and refilling the jugs with clean water.
When everyone has finished:

Leader   Jesus said, 'Do you understand what I have just done to you? If I your Lord and teacher have washed your feet, then you must wash each other's feet.'

PRAYER

Leader   I invite anyone who would like to, to say a prayer now if they wish. After each prayer let's all say 'Amen'.

Let us sit quietly now for a few minutes, with no talking, simply listening to God's voice within us.

Allow a short time of silence, judging how long is appropriate for the group.

Leader	To end our prayer time, let's say the Lord's Prayer together as we hold hands around the circle. ...... *(Name)*, would you like to start the prayer?

FINAL SONG *'Ewe Thina' (We walk his way) South African song.*
It is advisable to sing this in English so all understand the words.

Leader	We have been thinking about feet. What footprint do we take home with us today? We have received something through washing each other's feet, and we have given something. This is mutuality. Each of us can give, each of us can receive. Each of us can help someone else. Each of us can allow ourselves to be helped by someone else. We need each other. Each of us has a gift, each of us needs the other. Do you remember we thought about this when we looked at the story of Mary visiting her cousin, Elizabeth?

CELEBRATION

Share an agape meal with bread and grape juice or wine.

9   The Cross

Aim

To help people understand what happened at the crucifixion.

You will need

Props

- A large Bible.
- A full-sized cross – the height of a person – made of lightweight pinewood so it is not too heavy to carry. It could be painted black.
- A large black cloth to be hung to create a tomb.
- A hammer and three nails.
- A crown of thorns.
- A long stick with a sponge tied on to the end.

Actors

God – white cloth, or a white alb.
Jesus – a white cloth or cloak.
Three soldiers – leather belts, sticks.
John – a coloured cloth.
Mary and other women – shawls.
Joseph of Arimathea – a prayer shawl or
a cloak.

Preparation

- Rehearse the actors if possible, or have
  people who can support and guide
  them.
- Decide where the gathering will be for
  part 1 and part 2: in the same room as
  usual, or in a church. Ensure people are
  informed the week before where the
  gatherings will be.
- Work out how to create a 'tomb' in the space you are gathering in. One sugges-
  tion is to hang a large black cloth from a washing line in one corner.

Decoration

Empty the space as much as possible of decorations; have low lights and dark colours; have the tomb ready in place at the front where all can see it.

WELCOME

ACTIVITY AND PRAYER

PART 1

This could take place sometime during the day.

SONG   'Come all you people, come and praise your maker',
              Zimbabwean song.

EXPLANATION OF THEME

Leader   On Palm Sunday in church, we remembered Jesus going into Jerusalem on a donkey and the crowd shouting out, 'Hosanna to the king!' Then on Holy Thursday we remembered the last meal Jesus had with his friends before his death: how he washed their feet, how he told them to love one another as he had loved them, and how he shared bread and wine with them saying it was his body and blood.

On Good Friday some of us go to church and remember how Jesus died on the cross. All these stories are in the Bible, the book which tells us stories about God, about Jesus and about the Holy Spirit. In the Bible we read how much God loves us. Today we are going to look at the story in the Bible of how Jesus died. But remember, he rose again and is alive now. Here is our Bible.

BREAKING OPEN THE WORD

Leader   'God loved the world so much that he sent his only son, Jesus, to live with us, so that whoever believes in Jesus should not die but live for ever with God.' *(John 3.16)*

SONG   *'Wa wa wa emimimo (emioloye)' (Come, Holy Spirit, come, come, come), Nigerian song.*

Reading   John 19.16–30

Leader   After his last meal with his friends Jesus was arrested and tried. He was condemned to death. So soldiers took Jesus …

Three soldiers take hold of Jesus' arms.

Leader   And made him carry his own cross to a place called Golgotha.

The soldiers gesture to the cross and get Jesus to carry it. They lead Jesus around the room to the place which will be Golgotha.

Leader   There they nailed him to a cross.

They lean the cross against the wall. Two soldiers may need to hold the arms of the cross in place until the end of the drama. The third places Jesus' hands in place and hammers against the wood in such a way as to make a noise but avoiding hitting Jesus! Two soldiers may have to support the cross and Jesus' arms.

Leader   Under the cross stood Mary, the mother of Jesus, and John, the friend he loved and other women who loved Jesus.

Mary, John and other women stand at the foot of the cross and look sorrowful.

Leader   Jesus said, 'I'm thirsty.'

A soldier offers a stick with a sponge tied to its end to Jesus.

Leader   A few hours later Jesus said, 'It is finished,' and he died.

Jesus bows his head.

Leader   A man called Joseph who came from Arimathea took down Jesus'
          body and buried it.

*The soldiers find a way to take Jesus off the cross and put him behind the tomb
cloth, leaving the cross on the ground at the front, in the centre.*

Leader   This is the Word of the Lord.
All   **Amen.**
Leader   I invite you now to sit quietly and pray in silence if you wish, or to
          leave quietly. For those who can, we will meet again this evening
          at ... o'clock here.

PART 2

This could take place in the evening.

Aim

To allow people to reflect on the cross and on the love of Jesus for each one of us.

You will need

Props

- A large Bible.
- A large cross laid on the floor, preferably the one used earlier in the day, i.e. a
  cross the height of a person – made of lightweight pinewood.
- Battery tea lights at each corner of the cross.
- A hammer.
- Three nails.
- A CD of Taizé chants suitable for Good Friday.
- Possibly the potential to play 'Jesus' blood never failed me yet' *by Gavin Bryars
  with Tom Waits (see YouTube).*

Preparation

- Choose three people to each say a prayer. They must be able to do actions which people can clearly mirror.
- Ask three people to share for about five minutes or less on what the cross means to them in their life. It would be good to have a mix of people, e.g. women / men; old / young; new people / long-term people / people with a learning disability...
- Ask three pairs (each a person with and a person without a learning disability) to hammer a nail into the cross (where the hands and feet of Jesus would be).

Set-up

- Seats in a circle with the cross laid on the floor in the centre.
- Some cushions in front of the chairs for those who might like to sit on the floor.
- Low lights, no decorations.

PRAYER

EXPLANATION OF THEME

Get everyone to sit in a circle round the cross, on chairs and floor cushions.

Leader   Let us gather now round the cross. Imagine how the friends of Jesus felt after seeing him die on the cross and then seeing him buried. We are going to take some time now to think of Jesus, to remember how much he loves us and to ask him to carry for us any difficulties and sorrows we have at the moment.
Let's begin by singing:

SONG   *'Look around you, can you see?' by Jodi Page-Clark.*

During the song place four tea lights in glasses at each point of the cross. Not on the cross, as they will jump when nails are hammered in.

Note: *Fire safety: if real tea lights are used and not battery ones, then appoint a 'fire safety person' who will watch these candles throughout the prayer around the cross, to make sure people do not set fire to their hair or anything else! This person can also check no one gets their eyes too close to nails!*

Leader   This evening we remember the death of Jesus on the cross and his burial.
(*If your gathering is on Good Friday then the leader can say:* 'Tomorrow those who wish could pray at the cross in the church/ here. Take some flowers to the cross tomorrow if you wish. Then

finally we will celebrate on Sunday his rising from death with a celebration lunch together.')

This evening, three people are going to share about the meaning of the cross in their lives and some people will hammer nails into the cross. After this there will be a time of singing and those who wish can pray at the cross.

But first, let us pray. There will be three prayers. Each prayer is followed by an action using our hands. I invite you to mirror what the person praying does.

Three prayers spoken by three different people:

First person   Lord, forgive us for when we have not loved as you want us to.

Cross fists on the chest then slowly release the fists and open out the hands.

All   **Lord, forgive us for when we have not loved as you want us to.**

Mirror the gestures.

SONG   *Kyrie eleison: from 'Look around you, can you see?'*

Second person   Lord, give us the strength we need to carry our own cross, to carry the difficulties in our own lives.

Look at your own cupped palms and reflect for a few moments.

All   **Lord, give us the strength we need to carry our own cross, to carry the difficulties in our own lives.**

Mirror the gestures.

SONG   *Christe eleison: from 'Look around you, can you see?'*

Third person   Lord, help us to give our life for other people.

Offer cupped hands as if giving a gift.

All   **Lord, help us to give our life for other people.**

Mirror the gestures.

SONG   *Kyrie eleison: from 'Look around you, can you see?'*
                      'Behold the wood of the cross' by Daniel L. Schutte.

Leader   We will now hear a story from the Bible, the book which tells us stories about God, about Jesus and about the Holy Spirit. In the Bible we read of how much God loves us. This is the story of how Jesus was buried.

Reading   Matthew 27.57–61

Leader   In the evening after Jesus had died on the cross, a rich man called Joseph went to Pilate, the Roman leader, and asked for the body of Jesus so he could bury it properly. Joseph was from a place called Arimathea and had become a follower of Jesus.

Pilate ordered the body to be given to Joseph. So Joseph took the body, wrapped it in a clean white cloth and put it in his own new tomb which he had carved out of the rock. He then rolled a large stone across the entrance of the tomb to shut it and went away. Two women who loved Jesus, Mary Magdalen and another woman also called Mary were there, sitting opposite the tomb. They saw where Jesus was buried.

Nails should be given to the people who will be supporting the people with learning disabilities to hammer them into the cross. The hammer should be held by the first support person, then passed directly into the hands of the second support person, who passes it to the third support person at the right time. The hammer must not be left lying on the floor at any point as there is potential for both distraction and danger!

SONG   *'Behold the wood of the cross' by Daniel L. Schutte (chorus, v. 1, chorus).*

Nail   *Wait for singing to finish then first pair hammer a nail into the cross.*

Sharing 1   First person shares about the meaning of the cross to them.

SONG   *'Behold the wood of the cross' (chorus, v. 2, chorus).*

Nail   *Wait for singing to finish then second pair hammer a nail in.*

Sharing 2   Second person shares about the meaning of the cross to them.

SONG   *'Behold the wood of the cross' (chorus, v. 3, chorus).*

Nail   *Wait for singing to finish then third pair hammer a nail in.*

Sharing 3   Third person shares about the meaning of the cross to them.

SONG   *'Behold the wood of the cross' (chorus, v. 4, chorus).*

A time of adoration around the cross. It is helpful to ask three confident people to begin the adoration modelling what is possible to do: kneeling and touching the cross, putting one's head on the cross, simply sitting nearby and touching the cross.

The adoration can be accompanied by appropriate Taizé songs such as:

- *'Adoremus te Domine'.*
- *'In manus tuas'.*
- *'Ubi caritas'.*
- *'O Christe, Domine Jesu'.*
- *'Jesus, remember me, when you come into your kingdom'.*

Note: *Musicians need to be prepared to continue songs for quite a long time each. People may or may not join in with the singing. If/when the singing peters out, have instrumental music either live or taped (for this compile and use a CD of Taizé chants for Good Friday with no alleluias).*

You could finish by playing 'Jesus' blood never failed me yet'.

At some point two people could lift the cross and take it to people in wheelchairs, to those who cannot kneel and to those who find it hard to move once safely seated. This allows them to touch the cross and nails and pray if they wish. This is particularly helpful for those with visual impairment.

Once everyone has spent the time they want to at the cross, two or three people can carry it out quietly and solemnly. If it is Good Friday, then the cross could be taken to an appropriate place to be available for prayer on Holy Saturday. The candles can remain and the lights kept low so that those who wish can continue to pray quietly in the silence. People can be encouraged to leave quietly, and go straight home rather than staying and chatting.

10   Transformation

Aim

To help people understand that life can come even through times of great suffering, loss and difficulty.

You will need

Props

- Green cloth strips – enough for each person.
- Leaves.
- Rice grains in a basket – enough for a hand-ful for each person.
- Long blue cloths – to create flowing water.
- Bowls.
- A hollow bamboo stick.
- Laminated leaf shapes with *'The leaves of the tree are for the healing of the nations'* Rev. 22.2 on one side *(See Appendix 5)*.

Actors

The king – rich cloth.
Bamboo tree (two people) – green cloths, brown trousers.
The Wind – blue and / or white cloths.
Two narrators: one for the king, one for the bamboo and the narration.

Decoration

- If possible have a bamboo plant at the entrance to the gathering place.
- A tree (this could be bare branches stuck in a pot) front centre with the laminated leaf shapes hanging from the branches, and bowls of water at the foot.

Preparation

- Make the cards.
- Rehearse the main actors.

WELCOME

As people enter give each one a strip of green cloth and invite them to keep these safe for when they will be needed.

GATHERING SONG

'Come all you people, come and praise your maker', Zimbabwean song.

ACTIVITY AND PRAYER

EXPLANATION OF THEME

Leader	Today we are going to hear a story from the Far East. The story is not from the Bible but the meaning is the same as you can find in Bible stories. It is about how God can bring life for all, even through great suffering and sacrifice. It shows us that even at a time when we think we have lost everything, God can work all things together for the good of those he loves. In other words, God can make good things happen from even painful, difficult times in our lives.

BREAKING OPEN THE WORD

Reading

A LEGEND FROM THE FAR EAST: THE BAMBOO TREE

Leader	Let's listen together to a story.
Narrator 1	Once upon a time, there was a beautiful garden. And each evening, in the cool of the day, the king loved to walk in his garden. Of all the plants, flowers and trees in the garden, the most beautiful was Bamboo. Year after year, Bamboo grew even more beautiful. He knew he was loved by the king. He knew the king delighted in him. He was happy and proud to be so loved by the king.
	Could you all raise your arms and become trees in the garden?
	Can you make the sound of birds singing?

The king walks among all the trees (the audience) and admires them, especially Bamboo.

Bamboo	Often when Wind came to play in the garden, Bamboo would dance and sway happily, tossing and leaping and bowing joyfully. He would lead all the other trees in a dance which the king loved to watch.
Narrator	Can you make the sound of the wind? And dance as the trees in the wind?

The Wind blows through the trees. The trees, especially the Bamboo, sway and dance. The king watches and looks delighted.

Narrator	One day the king came to see his Bamboo. And Bamboo, full of love, bowed to the ground with joy. The king said, 'Bamboo, I would like to use you.'

The king and the Bamboo Tree speak – and react according to the narration below (with delight or horror, etc.).

Bamboo	Bamboo flung his head to the sky full of joy. The day had finally come when he could do something for his king! With great delight he said, 'Lord, I am ready, use me as you want.'
Narrator	'Bamboo,' the king said seriously, 'I would like to cut you down.'
Bamboo	Bamboo was horrified. 'Cut … me… down? But you love me; I'm the most beautiful tree in your garden. Please don't cut me down, oh, anything but that. Use me in any way that will give you joy, but please, please don't cut me down!'
Narrator	'I do love you Bamboo,' the king said even more seriously. 'But if I don't cut you down, then I cannot use you.'
Bamboo	The garden grew still. Wind held her breath. Bamboo slowly bent his proud head. Finally he whispered, 'Then, if you cannot use me unless you cut me down, then do what you want and cut me down.'
Narrator	The king said, 'Bamboo, beloved Bamboo, I also want to cut off your leaves and branches.'
Bamboo	Bamboo was sad. 'Lord, please don't! Cut me down if you must, but please don't take my leaves and branches also!'
Narrator	The king said, 'Bamboo, I am sorry but if I do not cut them away, I cannot use you.'
Bamboo	Bamboo shivered in fear but whispered, 'Lord, do with me as you want.'
Narrator	The king continued 'Bamboo, Bamboo, I want to divide you in two so that I can use you to give life to others.'
Bamboo	Bamboo quietly and sadly said, 'Lord, then cut and divide me in two.'

| Narrator | So the king took Bamboo and cut him down. He hacked off his branches. He stripped off his leaves. He divided him in two. |

The king mimes cutting Bamboo down – the two people who are the Bamboo tree move away from each other.

| Narrator | Then, lifting him gently, the king carried him to where there was a spring of fresh, sparkling water. He put one end of broken Bamboo into the spring and the other end into his dry field of rice. |

The king lays Bamboo down. The two people lie side by side so their heads are where the blue water cloths lie and their feet point towards the audience, the 'dry fields of rice'.

| Narrator | The clear, sparkling water from the spring flowed down the channel of Bamboo's opened body into the waiting fields where rice was going to be planted. |

Two people ripple a blue cloth down over the two people who are the Bamboo and now form a pipe, and into the audience.

| Narrator | Then rice was planted. |

The king mimes planting rice walking among the audience by putting some grains of rice into each person's hand.

| Narrator | Days went by. The shoots grew ever taller and stronger. |

The audience raise the green strips (the paddy) they were given as they came in.

| Narrator | After some weeks, the harvest was ready. |

The audience raise the rice they have just been given as the harvest.

| Narrator | On that day Bamboo, who was once so proud and beautiful, became even more beautiful in giving life to others. By allowing himself to be used by the king, life in all its fullness could flow through him to the fields so that the rice could grow and become food for the people. Bamboo gave life to the world. |

PRAYER

Lay a blue cloth from the foot of the tree at the front and place a bowl. Then pour water down a hollow bamboo stick, into the bowl held over the blue cloth.

| Leader | I invite you now to come forward in your own time to wash your hands in the water in the bowl as a sign of accepting God's life. As we do this let's sing, 'Jesu, tawa pano', which means 'Jesu, we are here today for you'. |

SONG DURING ACTION

> '*Jesu, tawa pano' (Jesus, we are here for you) by Patrick Matsikenyiri.*

Reader   Revelation 22.1–2

> ... the river of life rose from the throne of God. On either side were the trees of life ... the leaves of which are for the healing of all peoples.

SONG   '*Thuma mina, thuma mina, thuma mina, somandla' by David Dargie.*
(You can make up other verses, e.g. Use me, Jesus; Love me, Jesus; Lead me, Jesus, Help me, Jesus ...)

Leader   I invite anyone who would like to, to say a prayer now if they wish. After each prayer let's all say 'Amen'.

Allow time for this.

Leader   Let us sit quietly now for a few minutes, with no talking, simply listening to God's voice within us.

Allow a short time of silence, judging how long is appropriate for the group.

Leader   To end our prayer time, let's say the Lord's Prayer together as we hold hands around the circle ...... *(Name)* would you like to start the prayer?

FINAL SONG '*Amen themba' by John L. Bell.*

CELEBRATION

Eat rice salads.

Invite people to take a leaf shape with a quote on it from the tree as they leave.

11 Celebration

Aim

To encourage people to celebrate …

You will need

Actors

- The king – a crown or a gold turban, a rich cloak (choose someone who can be relied upon to make very expressive and clear facial expressions).
- The bride – White cloths and flowers.
- The son (bridegroom) – Purple cloth.
- Servants – White napkins over their forearms, plain coloured or striped aprons, or coloured cloth draped round shoulders.
- A narrator.
- A musician.
- A signer.

Props

- A large Bible.
- A long cloth for a banquet table.
- Grapes in bowls.
- Juice and plastic glasses.
- Basket of bread.
- Cushions.
- Baskets of invitations (A8 cards with the painting of a feast by Harold Lejeune *(see p. 166)* on one side and quote 'Come to the feast' on the back).
- The icon of the Trinity.
- A beautiful cloth for prayer.
- Rich clothes/jewellery, e.g. tinfoil and tinsel to be twisted into bangles and necklaces.
- Poor clothes, e.g. black bin bags.
- Bowls of water – only to be used if time allows.
- Stones – only to be used if time allows.

Preparation

- Rehearse the main actors.
- Make the invitations.

WELCOME

Have two people at the door welcoming and showing people where to sit as musicians teach songs, and play.

ACTIVITY AND PRAYER

Leader   Let's start our celebration with a song.

SONG   *'His banner over me' by Kevin Prosch.*

EXPLANATION OF THEME

Leader   Jesus came to give us good news. He came to tell us that we are *all* welcome in the kingdom of God; that God loves us each one of us just as we are and that God longs to share that love with us. He explained all this by telling stories. He was a great storyteller and today we are going to share with you one of his stories from the Bible. The Bible is the book which tells us stories about God, about

Jesus and about the Holy Spirit. In the Bible we read of how much God loves us.

We will need you all to help us so are you willing to take part? Choose whether you wish to be rich or poor and dress up. The rich should go to this corner, and the poor should go over there. Don't be shy!

Indicate where each group should go and allow time for people to choose their part and to settle.

Leader   The rich are going to get rich silver jewellery and cloths, and the poor are going to get – nothing! Except black bin bags! You have just five minutes to get dressed as a rich person, or as a poor person. Help each other if necessary!

Give people just five minutes to get dressed in character. The fun is in the spontaneity and the pressure of time. Too much time and people think too much and can get blocked trying to create something really 'good'. With just five minutes people know they have no time to be clever or to make anything perfectly, which is very freeing!

BREAKING OPEN THE WORD

Reading   Matthew 22.1–14

Leader   There was once a king.

The king steps forward.

Leader   He was a rich king who was generous and good.
He had a son.

The son steps forward.

Leader   His son was in love with a beautiful woman …

The bride steps forward.

Leader   … and they were going to get married.

The son and the bride hold hands and look at each other.

Leader   The king decided to hold a great wedding feast for them. He told his servants to prepare the feast.

Servants lay the long cloth on the ground in the centre, to make a banquet table, then place glasses, flowers, grapes, bread, juice on it. Musicians play a song (instrumental only), e.g. 'Food, glorious food' from the musical 'Oliver!'.

Leader   Then the king sent his servants to invite the guests.

The king claps his hands and the servants run to him and bow. He gestures to send them to invite the rich and gives them baskets of invitation cards to give to the rich (the cards with an image of a banquet on them: see the list of props above)
As the servants invite the rich, sing the chorus, verse 2, and the last verse of 'Come to the banquet, there's a place for you' by Fay White.

Leader	But the rich people all gave excuses and refused to come to the feast.

Ask the rich to give their excuses. The rich will have to improvise their excuses spontaneously. Use a roving mike for this if necessary.

Leader	Now can we just stop a minute? Look, the banquet is all prepared, but now see how the king feels to have everyone refuse his invitation.

Point to the king so everyone looks at him and sees how sad he looks.

Leader	And now let us take a moment to reflect on the times we refuse the invitation to God's feast and why, what are our excuses?

Moment of silence to allow people time to reflect personally.

Leader	Then the king sent the servants to call all the poor, the lame, the blind, the homeless, the sick.

The servants invite the poor giving out the same cards the rich were given. As this happens sing the chorus of 'Come to the banquet' and some of the other verses.

Leader	Now let us stop and ask the poor how they feel to be invited?

Ask the poor to say how they feel to be invited to the king's feast (use a roving mike for this). The poor will have to improvise their responses spontaneously.

Leader	And now let us take a moment to reflect on who are the poor today, and what is our own poverty?

Moment of silence to allow people time to reflect personally.

Leader	Then the king, the bride and the groom welcomed the poor.

The poor come to the table. Play joyful music as they come to the table. Bring chairs for those who need them, and cushions to help others.

Leader	And how does the king feel now that the poor come to his feast?

Point to the king so everyone looks at him and sees how joyful he looks.

SONG	'Lord I lift your name on high' by Rick Founds.

Leader	And how do the rich feel – to be excluded?

Ask the rich to say how they feel not to be at the feast. They will need to improvise their responses.

Leader	What do they need to do to be included, to be welcomed into the feast?

Allow time for the rich who wish, to remove their rich clothes, to share their riches and to be welcomed at the feast.
Have a time of dancing and feasting with the bread, grapes and grape juice.
Then the servants remove the table, food and drink, and play some lively dance music, e.g. 'Twist and shout!', 'Rock around the clock tonight', 'Dancing Queen' …
End with the Israeli wedding dance (Nigun Atik which can be found on YouTube). The bride and groom could stand in the centre of the circle being blessed by the dancers.

Leader	And how does the king feel now that there is a true celebration where everyone is welcome? And how does everyone else feel?

Allow time for anyone who wants to, to respond.

SONG	*Repeat 'Lord I lift your name on high' by Rick Founds.*

PRAYER

The king holds a large candle high and goes into the centre of the room. He places the candle in the centre on the floor. An icon could be used instead.

Leader	Let us pray. Let's begin with a short reading:

Reading   Luke 14.12–14

Leader	Jesus said, 'When you have a feast, a really good meal, do not invite your friends or your family or rich neighbours, in case they invite you back. But when you give a feast, invite people who are poor, lame, or blind. Then you will be blessed. Then you will be happy.' This is the Word of the Lord.
All	**Amen.**

EXPLANATION OF THE THEME

Leader	Jesus said that the kingdom of God is like a wedding feast and at a wedding feast everyone eats well! People are happy, they dress up beautifully, there is music and rejoicing. It is a true celebration. That is what God wants for us – that we know we are loved, that we are welcome and that he wants to celebrate with us.

If time allows, continue with the section between *…*; if not, leave it out.

*****Leader**	Let us take a few moments now to ask forgiveness of God for the times we refuse his invitation to celebration. We will do this in silence as we reflect on our excuses to God for not accepting his invitation to his celebration. It may be because we are too self-centred, or because we are too busy, or because we are too focused on our own worries and don't trust God enough. In your own time, you might like to take a stone to hold as you reflect.

Allow time for people to take a stone.

Leader	Feel the weight of the stone, its coldness, its hardness.

Allow time for this.

Leader	When you are ready and if you wish, place the stones in the bowl of water in the centre as a sign of asking God for forgiveness, of letting go what is hard, of asking to be washed clean.

During this action sing meditative Taizé chants, e.g. 'Ubi caritas …' or simply quiet instrumental music. *

Leader	I invite anyone who would like to, to say a prayer now if they wish. After each prayer let's all say 'Amen'.

Allow time for people who wish to say a prayer.

	Let us sit quietly now for a few minutes, with no talking, simply listening to God's voice within us.

Allow a short time of silence, judging how long is appropriate for the group.

Leader	To end our prayer time, let's say the Lord's Prayer together as we hold hands around the circle. …… *(Name)* would you like to start the prayer?

FINAL SONG *Repeat 'Come to the banquet, there's a place for you'.*

CELEBRATION

The banquet has already been enjoyed! Send people home with a sweet – at least symbolically! Or take time to sit and share a really good meal. If so, sing a lively, joyful grace.

12   Gifts

Aim

Aim: to celebrate the gift of the Holy Spirit; to understand each other's gifts and celebrate our difference and interdependence; unity in our diversity.

You will need

Props

- A large Bible.
- A basket containing small cards in the shape of flames *(see Appendix 5)*.
- The ingredients for a cake (see the instructions below), a bowl and wooden spoon.
- The Paschal candle.
- Small tea light – one per person plus a small holder if possible (it is worth investing in tea light holders for other celebrations).
- Matches.
- Two baskets.

Preparation

• Write the name of each person on a separate 'flame card'.

For Prayer Alternative 1:
• Make fruit-shaped cards *(see Appendix 5)* and write a gift of the Holy Spirit on each one.
• Make slips of paper each with the name of someone in the group written on it.
• Small dish of oil perfumed with essential oil.

Central decoration for the prayer time

• Flame-coloured cloths to symbolize the flames of the Holy Spirit (see the photo for an example). These can be laid on the ground in the shape of a flame.
• A cut-out image of a dove – symbol of the Holy Spirit *(see Appendix 5)*.
• A flame coloured or white candle – with a red heart on it if possible.
• OR an A4 laminated sheet of the painting of Pentecost *(see p. 172)*.
• A Bible.

WELCOME

GATHER WITH MUSIC, e.g. *'Come now Holy Spirit'* by Peter Kearney, *www. peterkearneysongs.com.au.*

Welcome people, especially visitors, to the celebration and explain what will happen.

EXPLANATION OF THEME

By the leader putting questions and coaxing answers from the group reminding them of how the followers of Jesus would have felt:

Leader	Who remembers what happened to Jesus on Good Friday?
Leader	Where was Jesus on Holy Saturday?
Leader	What happened on Easter Sunday?
Leader	What was that like for his friends?
Leader	What has been happening for the 40 days since then? What stories have we been listening to in church these past weeks?

Leader	But for now, Jesus wants us to continue his mission of telling everyone of God's love for us. And to help us fulfil this important mission he is sending us the Holy Spirit, full of the gifts we need. For Christians, the feast of Pentecost is the day we welcome the Holy Spirit with a big celebration. We will hear the story of how Jesus' friends stopped being afraid, and became full of confidence and courage together. Before Pentecost, they felt lost. When the Holy Spirit came, they suddenly felt inspired and empowered. Inspired? This means being filled inside with the Spirit. Once the friends of Jesus received his Holy Spirit, they had the confidence and the sense of power to go out and tell others how much God loves them.
	Remember how lost, afraid and broken the friends of Jesus had felt when Jesus had died? Pentecost changed all that, transforming them, changing them into people of hope and love, ready and eager to tell everyone they met the story of Jesus and of God's love for each one of us.
	Pentecost is the story of the birth of the church of Jesus, so today we are going to have a birthday cake for the church!

Bring in the materials to make a birthday cake for the church. Each person in the group could bring a different ingredient to add, taking it in turns to stir the mixture.

There are three suggested ways to prepare the cake:

1 Before the gathering, ask different people to bring ingredients to make a cake: flour, eggs, butter, sugar, milk ...

Leader	We each have a gift to offer. You have each brought something needed for our cake.
	We need to come together to make the cake, just as we need to come together to make a community. Once we have everything we need to make the cake everything needs to be stirred in, just as we are stirred together in community – and it isn't always easy to be stirred up!
	Who wants to have the first turn to stir the cake?

Allow each to have a turn at stirring.

Leader	Now everything is stirred together we have a lovely cake mix. This can now be baked in the fire and heat of the oven to be transformed, changed, into a cake.

It could then be baked to be eaten at the closing celebration (or in Blue Peter style, you could have a cake 'already prepared and ready to eat'!)

2 Each household brings a layer of the cake having been given the following instructions: 'Make a layer of a cake. It is up to you to decide on the size, shape and flavour!' One household needs to be asked to bring something to decorate the top of the cake. Another household could be asked to bring something for the filling between each layer.

The different offerings are then assembled, probably with much laughter as no layer of the cake will be alike! But difference is needed in community. Variety is the spice of life!

3 Instead of taking time to make the cake together, have a ring cake and in the centre place the Paschal candle, symbol of Jesus alive and present today at the heart of the world.

Leader   The Holy Spirit is the power that was in Jesus, which he wants to give to everyone, everywhere, at all times. At Pentecost the Holy Spirit came as tongues of fire resting above the head of each of his friends. The Paschal candle is a symbol of Jesus alive in the world today spreading his light. You are now invited to come forward and light a candle from the Paschal candle. This is a sign of the power and light of Jesus which he wants to give to each of us. It is a reminder of the tongues of fire which rested on each friend of Jesus at Pentecost.

Each person lights their tea light from the Paschal candle.

Leader   Hold your light up – like the tongues of fire that were sent to rest on each friend of Jesus at Pentecost. The power Jesus gives us helps us to love, to forgive, to be kind, to be a light in the world. See the light you now hold, and all the light that is now in the room.

All hold their tea lights up.

Leader   Now you are invited to put your candles around the cake.

Each one puts their candle (tea light) around the cake in a tea light holder to avoid wax spilling.

Leader   See how the light is stronger when the candles are close together? When we are together as friends of Jesus we are stronger.
The Holy Spirit gave the friends of Jesus the ability to talk to people from many different countries about God and his son, Jesus, and their love for everyone. The day they received the Holy Spirit they spoke in many languages. How many languages can you say 'Hello' in? Can we learn to say 'Hello' in several languages now?

See what languages are present or teach 'Hello' in several languages:
French – Salut
German – Hallo
Spanish – Hola!
Italian – Ciao!
Hindi – Namaskar

Leader   So now every year at Pentecost we celebrate the birthday of the church and the beginning of people going out into the world to talk of Jesus and share his love and joy. Let's sing.

SONG   *'Over my head, I hear music in the air' arranged by John L. Bell.*
You could add your own verses, e.g.
'I hear Name and Name (people in the group)'
'I hear laughter in the air.'

BREAKING OPEN THE WORD

Leader   Today we are going to hear the story from the Bible of what happened after Jesus rose from the dead and went back to his Father in heaven. It is the story of how the friends of Jesus were given the Holy Spirit. The Bible is the book which tells us stories about God, about Jesus and about the Holy Spirit. In the Bible we read of how much God loves us.

Reading   Acts 2.1–4

When the feast of Pentecost came, fifty days after Jesus had risen from the dead, his friends were all together in one place. They were still fearful and had no confidence. Without warning there was a sound like a strong wind.

Encourage people to make the sound of wind.

Leader   No one could tell where it came from. It filled the whole building. Then, like a wildfire …

Encourage people to make gestures like flames and the sound of fire

Leader   … the Holy Spirit spread through them all, and they started speaking in a number of different languages.
What languages do you all speak? Can you all say something in your own language now, all at the same time? We could say: 'Jesus is alive. God loves us.'

Allow time for this.

They received the gifts of the Holy Spirit. Each of them became full of confidence and joy. They were changed, transformed. They wanted to share the good news that God loves us with everyone they met. They were full of joy and passion.

This is the Word of the Lord.

All   **Amen.**

TIME OF SILENCE

Leader   In pairs (or threes, or small groups depending on the number of people present) take time now to share (choose one or two topics from the list below to reflect on, depending on the group, or choose a different topic each year for the group's celebration of Pentecost):

- Look at the painting of Pentecost by Masaichi Wakamoto (*see p. 172*). He is an artist who has learning disabilities. Speak about what you see and how it makes you feel.
- The Holy Spirit came as fire at Pentecost. Talk about 'Brother Fire' as St Francis called it, and its gifts: warmth, power, life giving …
- Talk about the other symbols of the Holy Spirit and their gifts: breath, wind, the dove.
- When have you known love, joy and peace, the gifts of the Spirit, in your own life and in your family and friendships?
- Where have you shown love, joy and peace in your own life, and in your family and friendships?
- The Holy Spirit brings unity in diversity. How are people around you different? Man/woman, young/old …
- What unites you? What has brought you together today? What does it mean to be one in God?

Allow enough time for sharing in pairs, or threes or small groups.
Note: during this time blow out the candles (tea lights) so they can be lit again at the time of celebration when the cake will be eaten.

Leader   Can we come back together now into a circle? Would anyone like to say anything from their sharing time here in the big group?

Allow time for this.

PRAYER

Leader   Now let us take time to pray. Let us hold hands to show our unity. Who would like to start the Our Father? Today, if you speak another language, then pray the Our Father in your own language, or in another language that you know – all at the same time.

Hold hands and say the Lord's Prayer in as many languages as possible at the same time.

Leader   Have you noticed though we are many, we are one?
There are many languages in the world as we heard during the 'Our Father'. But there is one language we all speak and understand whether we use words or not, the one language of love. How can you show the language of love?

Listen to the responses.

Leader   One way to show the language of love is to exchange peace with one another. Let us do that now, and let us do it slowly, taking time with each person as we greet them and offer them peace. Receiving peace is like an anointing of the Holy Spirit.

Exchange peace with each other in the group.

Two alternatives are now given for the next part of the prayer. The second is shorter and simpler.

ALTERNATIVE 1

Leader   Another way to show the language of love is to share simple gifts. We talk of the gifts of the Holy Spirit. We are invited to share these gifts of the Holy Spirit with other people. In the centre you can see two baskets, one with fruit-shaped pieces of paper. Each fruit has a gift of the Spirit written on it. The other basket has bits of paper in it in the shape of a flame, representing the fire of the Spirit. Each one has the name of someone here today.
One by one, in your own time, pick one fruit, and one flame. If you pick a flame with your name then put it back in the basket and take another.

Each person takes a 'fruit' and a flame with a name on it.
A friend could quietly read out the gift and name for a partner if they need help with this.

Leader   You will also see in the centre a small bowl of oil.

One by one, give the fruit you picked out to the person named on the card. Then anoint the hands or forehead of the person with the oil, saying:

'...... *(Name)* share the Holy Spirit's gift of ...... *(whatever gift was named on the fruit-haped piece of paper)* with all whom you meet. Amen.'

Some people may need support for this.

When everyone has been anointed:

Leader   Let us give thanks for these gifts of the Holy Spirit that nourish us and work in us daily, helping us to fulfil our mission. Let's hold up our gifts now so all can see them. May we be faithful this year to the gift we have been given and share these gifts with others. Amen.

All   **Amen.**

An extension of this activity might be to encourage people to continue to pray over the Pentecost season for the person whose name they drew. This person will be their 'Spirit-kin', a bit like Kris Kringles or Secret Santa during Advent.

ALTERNATIVE 2 (a simpler version needing no preparation):

Leader   Look at the person on your left. What gift of the Holy Spirit do you think they have? Take a few moments to think about it. Ask for help from someone else if you want.

It might help to ask people to call out the gifts of the Spirit to give examples of what they might see in another person. Add in suggestions of your own from the list below.

Leader   We are now going to affirm the gifts of the Holy Spirit in each other. I will start. I will turn to the person on my left and say:

'...... *(Name)*

We believe in you.

...... is your gift.

Share this gift from the Holy Spirit with everyone.

Amen.'

Then we will continue round the circle.

Ensure people who need help are supported to do this.

CONTINUATION OF THE PRAYER

Leader	Now let us take a time to give thanks for all the people we see as being filled with God's Spirit – those who have the gifts of the Spirit: love, joy, peace, patience, kindness, goodness, gentleness, faithfulness and self-control. You might like to name these people, our 'Pentecost friends', out loud.

Allow time for those who want to name such people. It can help by saying one name yourself, first e.g. Archbishop Desmond Tutu, the Dalai Lama, someone's mother, a friend who works in a hospital ...

Leader	Jesus, thank you for the Holy Spirit. Help us to spread the gifts of the Holy Spirit to all whom we meet. Amen.
All	**Jesus, thank you for the Holy Spirit. Help us to spread the gifts of the Holy Spirit to all whom we meet. Amen.**
SONG	*'You've gotta sing when the Spirit says sing', African-American spiritual.*
Leader	I invite anyone who would like to, to say a prayer now if they wish. After each prayer let's all say 'Amen'. Let us sit quietly for a few minutes, with no talking, simply listening to God's voice within us.

Allow a short time of silence, judging how long is appropriate for the group.

Leader	To end our prayer time, let's say the Grace together as we hold hands around the circle. ...... *(Name)* would you like to start the prayer?
All	**May the grace of our Lord Jesus Christ, the love of God and the fellowship of the Holy Spirit be with us now and evermore. Amen.**
SONG	*'Sing a new song unto the Lord ...' by Dan L. Schutte.*

CELEBRATION

You could make up your own verses e.g. 'and makes me clap/ laugh/ shout for joy'. Carry the cake and all the tea lights to the meal table and light the candles again. Have a joyous meal, a feast, e.g.

• *A flame-coloured meal, e.g. tomato soup, Leicester cheese on toast, tomato salad, orange and banana fruit salad ...*

OR

• *A meal with foods from different countries.*

OR

• *A bowl of lots of different fruits as a symbol of the fruits of the Spirit.*
OR
• *Simply a good meal.*

Finish the meal with the Pentecost birthday cake and sing:

'Happy Birthday to us, happy birthday to us, happy birthday to the church, happy birthday to us!'

Then all blow out the candles.

SONG   *'I am the church, you are the church' by Richard K. Avery and Donald S. Marsh.*

Continue the celebration with circle dancing where all interweave with energy in the joy of the Holy Spirit. Or use a compilation of Abba's greatest hits! There is a dance of love within the Trinity, a dance of relationship.

THE TIME OF DEPARTURE

Leader   Take a piece of the cake home with you to share with others.
And I invite each of you who wishes, to take your tea light home. It can represent the fire of the Holy Spirit which we have celebrated today. Take it into each room of your home, bringing the fire of the Holy Spirit there. You could say an appropriate prayer for each room, for example:
In a bedroom: May …… (Name) find the Holy Spirit's gift of peace and rest in their room. Amen.
In the entrance hall: May everyone who comes find the Holy Spirit's gift of welcome here. Amen.
In the kitchen: May the food cooked here give the Holy Spirit's gift of life and joy to all who eat it. Amen.

Each year at Pentecost the Daughters of the Holy Spirit Religious Congregation prepare slips of paper, each one with a gift of the Holy Spirit written on it (see below for their list). At the end of their Pentecost celebration, each person is invited to take one of the slips, and then to be aware of this gift in their lives in the coming year. You might like to do the same.

The gifts of the Holy Spirit named in Galatians 5.22–23:

Love	Patience	Gentleness
Joy	Kindness	Faithfulness
Peace	Goodness	Self-control

Other gifts:

Passion	Clarity	Obedience
Commitment	Surrender	Trust
Life	Expectancy	Purpose
Energy	Hope	Freedom
Confidence	Communication	Grace
Empowerment	Intuition	Truth
Awe and wonder in God's	Prophecy	Simplicity
presence	Enjoyment	Courage
Common sense	Good judgement	Tenderness
Play	Compassion	Delight
Faith	Enlightenment	Forbearance
Education	Hospitality	Enthusiasm
Mercy	Warmth	Balance
Faithfulness	Sense of humour	Strength
Knowledge	Integrity	Transformation
Wisdom	Perseverance	Healing
Understanding	Sincerity	Gratitude
Good counsel	Loyalty	Beauty
Holiness	Sympathy	Responsibility
Fortitude	Encouragement	Light
Forgiveness	Reverence	
Inspiration	Purity of heart	

APPENDIXES

Appendix 1

A glossary of 'church-speak' for all

Ways of explaining difficult words found in Bible readings and in worship to people with learning disabilities

Introduction

People with learning disabilities can have a limited vocabulary. But some words often used in church can be really hard to understand, even for theologians, let alone the rest of us. Hence this glossary. Our rule of thumb is to keep it simple, clear and concrete. If you are able to use an example or an image, so much the better. Some concepts (e.g. mercy) benefit from trying a variety of explanations, to help people grasp the idea behind the word.

As you speak with a person or group, be attentive to any sign of understanding. If you don't see a sign, don't be discouraged! It doesn't necessarily mean that the person has not understood. And even if some people with learning disabilities may never understand the words, your body language, tone of voice and way of engaging will convey the essential message: welcome, acceptance and belonging. As St Francis said, 'Preach the gospel at all times. Use words if necessary.' Use this list as a starting point for your own creativity to tell the story of God.

When trying to help your listeners to understand either a Bible passage or a theological concept, use simple language, short sentences, and keep checking that your listeners are following and keep trying until they seem to get what you are saying! Give examples if it helps.

When simply reading a Bible passage it is best, as far as possible, to substitute a complex word with a simple word, e.g. 'disciples' can become 'friends'.

Abba – Father, daddy, dad; this is how Jesus called God, his Father.

Abide – To live in one place for a long time; to stay joined to, to remain.

Adore – To sit lovingly with God.

Adultery – A husband's or wife's sexual relationship outside marriage.

Advent – The weeks before Christmas. This season begins on the fourth Sunday before Christmas. It is a time when we wait in joyful hope for Jesus to be born, and we think about God who will come again in glory.

Altar – The special table in a church where a priest celebrates the last meal Jesus had with his friends. At this meal he shared bread and wine with them saying, 'This is my body; this is my blood.' In the Old Testament, God's people used stone altars to mark a place where God did something great.

Amen – Yes! Let this happen. It's true.

Angel – A messenger of God.

Anoint – To pour oil on someone to show they have been chosen by God.

Apostles – The twelve men chosen by Jesus to be his closest followers. He sent them to share his good news of God's love.

Ascension – Forty days after Easter, Jesus returned to God, his Father. He promised to send us the Holy Spirit. The Holy Spirit gives us all the gifts we need to continue the work of Jesus on earth.

Ash Wednesday – This is the first day of Lent. Lent is the 40 days of preparation for Easter. On this day, the priest or minister marks our foreheads with ash in the shape of a cross. This is a sign of our deep desire to turn back to the love of God.

Atonement – When Jesus died on the cross, he broke down all the barriers between God and us, bringing God's peace to the world and us.

Baptism – This is a ceremony when water is poured on a person as a sign they are in God's family with Jesus. It has been called a 'spiritual tattoo' of Christ on our soul to show we belong to him.

Bible – The big book (in fact a collection of books) that tells the story of God's love for his people. The second part of the Bible tells the story of Jesus' life, death and resurrection, and how his friends carried on his work.

To bless – To ask God to be especially close to someone, to encourage them.

Christmas – On this day we remember Mary giving birth to Jesus, who is God's son.

Church – The big family created by Jesus who meet together to pray, worship God and encourage one another to follow Jesus together. The building where they meet is often also called a 'church' or 'chapel'.

Collect – A short prayer near the beginning of a church service.

Collection – The money that Jesus' followers give during a church service to support the work of the church.

Commandments – God's rules for how we should live in the way he wants, that is respecting each person and living a full and free life.

Commitment – Making a promise or a firm decision and sticking with it.

Communion – The blessed bread and wine which is shared by the followers of Jesus in a church service. Some churches believe that Jesus is especially present with us in the bread and wine, fully himself. Communion also means deep friendship with Jesus. It is the spirit of unity between his friends, bringing new life and hope.

Condemn – To say someone is guilty of a crime and should be punished.

Confess – To admit I have done something wrong and to say sorry. To tell others what I believe in.

Conscience – An inner voice that guides us to choose between right and wrong. An uncomfortable feeling inside when we know we have done something wrong. It warns us, making us want to change for the better.

Consecrate – To give up something important, like time, money or even one's life for God; in some churches, bread and wine are consecrated and offered to God, to ask him to make them become the body and blood of Jesus.

Convict – To find someone guilty, to make someone feel guilty for something wrong they have done.

Covenant – God's promise of loving friendship with us forever.

Covet – To want something that belongs to someone else.

Creation – The world and all it contains, including us, as well as the sun, the moon and the stars; everything God has made.

Crucifixion – The killing of Jesus by nailing him to a wooden cross.

Curse – To say and wish something terrible will happen to a person or people.

Deacon – A person chosen to help the priest and people in a church.

Dedicate – To offer something important, like time, money or even one's life for God.

Demon – A bad spirit who is against God and wants bad things to happen to us.

Devil – The leader of the bad spirits who fights against God, wants bad things to happen to us, and tempts us to do wrong.

Disciple – A friend of Jesus who wants to stay close to him, learning from him and following him and carrying out his mission in the world.

Easter – On this day we celebrate that Jesus rose from the dead. We celebrate that he is alive today.

Elder – A wise, experienced person; someone chosen to help the leader of a church.

Epiphany – On this day we remember the wise men who made a long journey to visit Jesus as a baby, showing how God wants all people to share his love.

Eucharist/Holy Communion – The church service, often on a Sunday, when Jesus' friends remember his life, death and resurrection, and in his memory share bread and wine that has been specially blessed.

Evangelist – A person who tells others the good news of Jesus. The earliest books about Jesus were written by Matthew, Mark, Luke and John. They are called the Evangelists. Their books are called Gospels.

Everlasting/eternal – For ever and ever; never ending, like God's love which goes on forever.

Evil – Something bad, harmful and wrong, coming from the devil which destroys anything that is good in the world.

Evil spirits – In the time of Jesus, when a person had epilepsy or a mental illness, people imagined that they had an evil spirit inside them. See also 'Demon', p. 187.

Faith – The trust in God and his promises to us that come to friends of Jesus as a gift of the Holy Spirit so they can share it with others.

Faithful – To be caring and loving no matter what happens, always being there for someone when they need you.

Famine – When there is not enough food to eat so people go hungry.

Fasting – Cutting down on what we eat or drink for a while, in order to be more aware of God and of people who are much poorer.

Fellowship – The love which the Holy Spirit invites us all to share as followers of Jesus.

Flesh – When used in a good sense: our bodies; Jesus, God's son, became flesh. When used in a negative sense: distractions, anything in us which makes us turn away from God's love.

Foolish – Doing something without thinking about the problems it might cause.

Forgive – To accept a person's apology after they have hurt you, or upset you.

Gentile – Anyone who is not a Jew.

Gifts of the Holy Spirit – Special gifts or talents given to people who follow Jesus by the Holy Spirit so they can serve others in a better way.

Glorify – To praise and adore God.

Glory – The beauty and greatness of God.

Good Friday – On this day, we remember that Jesus died on a cross loving us to the end.

Gospel – The good news that God loves us deeply and forever no matter what we do. Jesus' message of hope and of God's deep eternal love for us. One of the four books in the Bible by Matthew, Mark, Luke and John, that tell the story of Jesus' life, death and resurrection.

Grace – God pouring his love into us like a never-ending fountain of fresh, clean water; a free, generous gift from God no matter what we have done. A special prayer we say before a meal to thank God.

Guilt – The bad feeling we have inside when we have done something wrong.

Hallelujah/alleluia – A joyful shout of praise to God, like 'Praise the Lord!'

Hallow – To give great respect to God, e.g. 'Hallowed be thy name'.

Heaven – The perfect place of peace and joy where God would like us all to live.

Hell – A place without joy, love, peace, or rest.

Holy – Walking with God in God's way, with love, joy and forgiveness.

Holy Spirit – The Holy Spirit is God, living with the Father and his Son Jesus; the Holy Spirit is God's energy, always there when we need help and encouragement.

Hosanna – 'Save us now!'; a word used to praise Jesus, on Palm Sunday.

Hypocrite – A person who says one thing but does something else. A person who sees the wrong things other people do, but does not see the wrong things they do themselves.

Idol – A false god; anything that takes the place of God in our lives.

Idolatry – Believing in false gods made by people, rather than the true God.

Incense/frankincense – A sweet-smelling substance that is burned to praise God. One of the gifts given to the baby Jesus by the wise men.

Intercede/intercessions – To pray for someone else/prayers for other people.

Judge – A person chosen to help people settle their problems. God too can act as a judge, showing us how to live better lives.

Justice – Treating each person fairly.

Justify – To repair our relationship with God.

Kingdom – The people and land ruled by a king or queen.

Kingdom of God/kingdom of heaven – God's home of peace, joy and justice. He wants us to live with him in heaven for ever.

Lent – Forty days of preparation before Easter: a time to pray, fast and give to people in need.

Leper – A person with a terrible skin disease who was pushed out of their society because people were afraid of them.

Manger – A box that holds hay for cows to eat.

Manna – Special food sent by God to feed his people in the desert when they had nothing to eat and were hungry.

Maundy Thursday – On this day we remember that Jesus washed the feet of his friends and gave them the gift of sharing bread and wine to remember him. We remember that he asks us to love one another as he loves us.

Meek – A meek person is one who is working for justice, who is not afraid to be gentle and kind, but who is also strong and willing to stand up to injustice.

Mercy – Helping people who are weak and in need, and unable to help themselves; giving a person a second chance, believing in a person's ability to be good in spite of wrong or hurtful things they may have done.

Miracle – An amazing act of God that shows God's power over the world. Examples of miracles include Jesus healing a blind man, or when he fed 5,000 people with five loaves and two fish.

Mission – A special purpose God gives us in order to share his love for our world, for others and for the earth.

Mourn – To be very sad, especially after someone we love has died.

Obey – To decide to do what another person tells us to do.

Offertory – The moment during a Sunday church service when the bread and wine are taken up to the altar, along with the money given by people in the church at the collection.

Parable – A short story from everyday life that teaches an important spiritual truth: Jesus told many parables about the kingdom of heaven.

Passover – A Jewish feast to remind them how God rescued them from the Egyptians.

Pastor – The leader of a church.

Pasture – Open grassy places where sheep and cows can eat.

Pentecost – This was the moment 50 days after Jesus' resurrection when the Holy Spirit came down upon his followers, bringing them new life and courage. It is seen as the birthday of the church.

Persecution – This is when people are hurt in some way for believing in God or simply because they are different.

Pharisees – Members of a Jewish group in Israel at the time of Jesus; their way of keeping the religious laws very strictly led some of them to argue with Jesus.

Praise – To pray or sing to God with joy for all the good things God has done and is doing.

Prayer – Taking time to be present to God, listening and talking to God as a friend, sitting with God in silence, singing to God.

Preach – To speak to a group of people about God. To help them to understand the Bible stories so they can follow God better.

Prophecy – A warning from God about what the people are doing wrong.

Prophet – A person sent by God with a special message to guide his people on the right path.

Psalm – A poem, a prayer or a song to God in the Old Testament, the first part of the Bible.

Rabbi – A teacher of the Jewish law, often called 'master' to show them respect.

Reconcile – To make peace with someone, to make peace with God.

Redeem – To set someone free; Jesus sets human beings free from our sins and is called the Redeemer; the act of setting us free, by dying on the cross and rising again, is called redemption; he mends all that is broken in us so that we can live a full life.

Repent – To be sorry for doing something wrong; to turn back to God and ask him to forgive us, and help us live better in future.

Resurrection – This is what happens at Easter, when Jesus rises from the dead, making it possible for us to share in his love, joy and power.

Revelation – God showing himself in our daily lives, or sometimes through amazing experiences, so that we know God and his ways better. God showing himself to us through the Bible.

Righteousness – To be in a loving relationship with God and with each other.

Sabbath – In the Bible, the Sabbath is the seventh day of creation: God made the world in six days and rested on the seventh day. A day of the week given to God in a special way, for rest, prayer and play. For Jews this is Saturday, for Christians it is Sunday. For many people it is quality family time.

Sackcloth – In the Bible we read of people putting on sackcloth and ashes. Sackcloth was scratchy poor material that people wore to show they were sad and sorry for their sins and that they wanted to turn back to God.

Sacrament – A special sign of God's love such as baptism and the Eucharist or Holy Communion. A special meeting place with God that gives us life.

Sacred – Something that is very special and holy. Something given to God and touched by God's presence.

Sacrifice – Something valuable and precious given to God in order to give thanks or to ask God for something. It was often placed on an altar by a priest, e.g. long, long ago, lambs were killed and offered to God as a sacrifice. A gift I love that I give up in order to be free to follow God.

Sadducees – A group of Jewish people at the time of Jesus who did not believe in life after death.

Saint – Anyone who loves God so much they want to be a close friend of Jesus and to live as he lived: loving, celebrating and forgiving as Jesus did. The Roman Catholic Church has named some very holy people as saints. They are an example to us of how to follow Jesus, e.g. St Francis of Assisi.

Salvation – Jesus died on the cross, out of love for us, so that we might be saved. Enjoying salvation is about coming home to God by accepting Jesus' forgiveness to us for all we have done wrong.

Sanctify – to make someone or something holy.

Sanctuary – The holiest place in a church where people gather to worship God. A place of safety.

Sanhedrin – At the time of Jesus the council of the most important Jewish religious leaders which was in charge of any religious matters.

Saved, to be saved – Jesus bringing us home to God. Jesus mending what is broken in us. Jesus enabling us to share in and enjoy God's life. To be given fullness of life that never ends.

Saviour – Jesus, who saves us and gives us new life with God.

Scripture – God's written word – the Bible. The story of God and God's love for us.

Seer – Someone who can see into the future. A prophet.

Sin – Turning away from God and choosing not to love; not to live and love as God wants us to live and love. Doing what is wrong.

Soul – The deepest part of us; our true self; our heart of hearts.

Spirit – The life of God in us. God's breath of life in us.

Synagogue – A building where Jews gather to worship God.

Tabernacle – In Roman Catholic churches: the special 'box' where Jesus is present in the form of bread that has been specially blessed in mass. For the Jews in the Old Testament, this was a holy tent where God met with his people.

Tax Collector – Someone working for the government to collect money from the people. In the time of Jesus such people were hated because they took money for themselves. The Gospel of Luke tells the story of Zacchaeus, the tax collector who changed his life after meeting Jesus.

Temple – The large building in Jerusalem where Jews worshipped God.

Temptation – A thought that tries to get us to do something wrong.

Testament – An agreement between God and his people. The Bible has two parts, the Old Testament and the New Testament: together, they tell the story of God's love for all people.

Throne – A special seat which only a king or queen is allowed to sit on.

Tithe – An offering to God to show that we are grateful.

Tomb – A place where a dead person is buried.

Transfiguration – The moment on a mountain when Peter, James and John saw Jesus shining with God's light: 'God all lit up!'

Tribe – To be a member of a tribe is to be part of a large family, whose roots go back many hundreds of years; there were 12 tribes in Israel, the descendants of the 12 sons of Jacob.

Trinity – The loving relationship at the heart of God who is always Father, Son and Holy Spirit. God's Son became the man, Jesus.

Unclean – Not clean, not pure. Something that the Jewish people were not allowed to use or to touch as it separated them from God.

Vocation – The way God calls each person to follow and be a friend of Jesus.

Wisdom – To know the difference between right and wrong, and between good and bad – and to choose what is right and good. To be able to understand the way things are and then to do or say the right thing. To see, speak and act as God would.

Witness – To tell others about Jesus. To tell others that God loves them.

Worship – To praise, adore, honour and glorify God through songs, prayers, dance, celebration or silence.

Appendix 2

Songs

TOWARDS INCLUSIVE CHURCH SERVICES

'Peace before us', David Haas © 1987 GIA Publications, Inc.
'You are the face of God', Karen Drucker (find on YouTube)

CHURCH SERVICES

1 The call of Abraham

'Bush Beatitudes', Noel Davis/John Coleman ©1998.
   See pp. 199–200 for the lyrics. For the music contact: colemansongs@yahoo.com.

2 The call of Moses

'This is holy ground; we're standing on holy ground', Christopher Beatty © 1982.
   Birdwing Music (ASCAP)/BMG Songs (ASCAP) (both admin. by EMI CMG
   Publishing).
'Here I am Lord, is it I Lord?' Daniel L. Schutte © 1981, OCP Publications.
'Moses, take your shoes off, you're on holy ground', Jessy Dixon (YouTube).

3 The call of Mary

'Hail Mary, gentle woman', Carey Landry, © 1975, 1978. Published by OCP.

4 The Visitation

'The Magnificat' (Mary's song), from Peter Kearney's CD *How far to Bethlehem?*:
   www.peterkearneysongs.com.au.
'Tell out my soul, the greatness of the Lord', Timothy Dudley-Smith © 1962,
   renewal 1990 Hope Publishing Co.

5 The Presentation of Jesus in the Temple

'Revealing the holy' © John Coleman 1998.
   See p. 200 for the lyrics. For the music contact: colemansongs@yahoo.com.

6 The wedding at Cana

'Nigun Atik' (YouTube).
'Fill my cup, let it overflow', St Petersburg Songsters (YouTube).

7 The Samaritan woman

'Come to the water' © John B. Foley, SJ, and OCP Publications 1978.
'Let your living water flow over my soul', John Watson ©1986 Ampelos Music.

8 The Parable of the Sower

'Rejoice in the Lord always', oral tradition, Baptist Hymnal 2008 #586.
'All good gifts around us', *Godspell*.

9 Feeding of the 5,000

'Be still for the presence of the Lord', David Evans © 1986 Kingsway's Thankyou
   Music, admin. EMI Christian Music Publishing.
'Spirit of the living God, fall afresh on me', Daniel Iverson © St. 1 1935, 1963
   Birdwing Music (ASCAP).

10 The Raising of Lazarus

'Never give up, Bambelela', Traditional South African © 2002, JL Zwane Memorial
   Congregation.

'Miserere mei domine, miserere', Taizé.

'Look around you, can you see?', Jodi Page-Clark © 1971, Celebration.

'Behold, behold, I make all things new', John L. Bell © 1994, Iona Community, GIA Publications, Inc.

11 Call of Mary Magdalene

'Ubi caritas', Taizé.

'I saw Mary in the garden', Rowland Howarth (see pp. 200–1 for lyrics).

'Jesus Christ is risen today', Charles Wesley, public domain.

12 The Risen Jesus appearing by the lakeside

'Take this bread, eat this bread, eat, and never be hungry', Taizé.

SMALL GROUPS CELEBRATIONS

'He's got the whole world in his hands', African-American spiritual.

1 Building up the body

'Let there be love shared among us', Dave Bilbrough © 1979 Thankyou Music (admin. by Crossroad Distributors Pty. Ltd).

'One bread, one body, one Lord of all' © John B. Foley SJ, and OCP Publications 1978.

'Kumbayah my Lord', African-American spiritual.

'It's me, it's me, it's me that builds community' (The Community Song), www.youtube.com/watch?v=iQPTPa5XDPY

2 Light in the darkness

'Christ be our light, Shine in our hearts' © Bernadette Farrell 1993.

'Shine Jesus, shine', Graham Kendrick © 1987 Make Way Music.

'This little light of mine', Bob Gibson © The Bicycle Music Company.

3 Encouragement

'My spirit rejoices in my God' © Brian Halferty. See pp. 201–2 for the lyrics.
'The Lord hears the cry of the poor' John B. Foley SJ and New Dawn Music ©
   1978, 1990.

4 Welcome

'Come all you people, come and praise your maker', Alexander Gondo (Stanza 1 ©
   1986, World Council of Churches; Stanzas 2–3 © 1995, from 'With One Voice'/
   Augsburg Fortress).
'Come to the circle' © John Coleman. See p. 202 for the lyrics. For the music
   contact: colemansongs@yahoo.com.
'Come with me for the journey is long', South African traditional, tr. © Lutheran
   World Federation.

5 Searching and finding

'Nigun Atik', YouTube.
'I have the joy, joy, joy, joy down in my heart' by George W. Cooke, public domain.
'Give thanks with a grateful heart' © Warner/Chappell Music, Inc., CAPITOL
   CHRISTIAN MUSIC GROUP.

6 Forgiveness and Reconciliation

'Bind us together Lord', Bob Gillman © 1977 Thankyou Music (PRS) (admin.
   worldwide by EMI CMG Publishing excluding Europe, which is administered
   by kingswaysongs.com).
'Jubilate Deo', Taizé.
'Let there be love shared among us', Dave Bilbrough © 1979 Thankyou Music
   (admin. by Crossroad Distributors Pty. Ltd).

7 Discovering the most important thing

'We hold a treasure not made of gold', © John B. Foley, SJ and New Dawn Music,
   1975, 1978.
'I come like a beggar,' Sydney Carter © 1974 Stainer & Bell Ltd.
'I will sing, I will sing a song unto the Lord', Max Dyer © 1974, Celebration
   (admin. by Maranatha! Music c/o The Copyright Company, Nashville, TN). All
   rights reserved. International copyright secured.

8 Looking after each other

'God welcomes all', John L. Bell © 2008 WGRG, Iona Community (admin. GIA
  Publications, Inc).
'Amen, siakudumisa!' (Amen, sing praises to the Lord!), C. Molefe © 1991 Lumko
  Institute.
'Come Holy Spirit, Maranatha', John L. Bell © 1995, WGRG the Iona Community
  (Scotland) (admin. GIA Publications, Inc.).
'Ewe Thina' (We walk his way), South African song, trs. © 2003 Utryck (admin.
  Walton Music Corporation).

9 The Cross

Part 1

'Come all you people, come and praise your maker', Zimbabwean song, St. 1 ©
  1986, World Council of Churches; St. 2–3 © 1995, in *With One Voice*, Augsburg
  Fortress.
'Wa wa wa emimimo (emioloye)', Nigerian song, tr. © 1986 World Council of
  Churches.

Part 2

'Look around you, can you see?', Jodi Page-Clark © 1971 Celebration.
'Behold the wood of the cross' © 1976, Daniel L. Schutte and New Dawn Music.
'Jesus' blood never failed me yet', Gavin Bryars with Tom Waits (YouTube).

10 Transformation

'Come all you people, come and praise your maker', Zimbabwean song St. 1 ©
  1986, World Council of Churches; St. 2–3 © 1995, in *With One Voice*, Augsburg
  Fortress.
'Jesu, tawa pano' (Jesus, we are here for you), Patrick Matsikenyiri © 1990, 1996
  General Board of Global Ministries, license #1062.
'Thuma mina, thuma mina, thuma mina, somandla', David Dargie © 1984, Ultryck
  (admin. GIA Publications, Inc.).
'Amen themba', trs. John L. Bell © 2008 Wild Goose Resource Group, Iona Com-
  munity, Scotland, GIA Publications, Inc., exclusive North American agent.

11 Celebration

'His banner over me' © 1991, Mercy Publishing, Words and Music by Kevin Prosch.
'Come to the banquet, there's a place for you' Fay White ©, 1996 https://loddon-
    malleeuca.blogspot.com/p/fays-songs.html.
'Lord, I lift your name on high', Rick Founds, 1989.
'Nigun Atik', YouTube.
'Ubi caritas', Taizé chant, or other meditative chants.

12 Gifts

'Come now Holy Spirit', words and music by Peter Kearney. Licensing through
    One Licence.
From Peter Kearney's CD "Make Me a Song…" Website: www.peterkearneysongs.
    com.au.
'Over my head, I hear music in the air', public domain (Google Over My Head,
    African-American spiritual arranged by John L. Bell) for the music.
'You've gotta sing when the Spirit says sing', African-American spiritual.
'Sing a new song unto the Lord…', Daniel L. Schutte © 1972. Published by OCP
    Publications; © 1972, 1974, 1979 OCP.
'I am the church, you are the church, we are the church together', Richard K. Avery,
    Donald S. Marsh © 1972 Hope Publishing Co.

LYRICS

Bush Beatitudes (suggested for the church service on the call of Abraham)

There are narrow tracks of invitation
That lead us to the virgin lands of God.

And we who dare – we can take them
And stumble slide and slip though we may.
Making new tracks through unknown
Learning the bush skills as we go.
And the angels at our side
Say 'on you go'.

On you go – on you go
On you go – on you go

This narrow track of invitation
Says travel light and be gentle as you go.

And share the swag with this hungry country,
Dig deep to forgive the ones who hurt you most.
And as you camp by the billabong
Let the campfire make you strong.
And hear the angels at your side
Say 'on you go'.

On you go...

And as you camp by the billabong
Let the campfire make you strong.
And hear the angels at your side
Say 'on you go'.

On you go...

And hear the angels at your side
Say 'on you go'.

CD *Revealing the Holy*, johncoleman.bandcamp.com/track/on-you-go-bush-beatitudes

Revealing the Holy (suggested for the church service on The Presentation of Jesus in the Temple)

Revealing the holy.
Revealing the holy.
In love we want to come.
Revealing the holy.
Revealing the holy.
In love we want to come.
Revealing the Holy One.

Enter the shadow
Enter though you may be walking blind
Enter the night - enter the sign

Chorus

In weakness our God is revealed
The wound must be opened before it will heal
Let's open our hearts and open the meal.

Chorus

At table we'll break and share bread.
Jesus says "When strangers are welcomed, I'm fed."
The humble will lead, and the proud shall be led.

Chorus

CD *Revealing the Holy*: johncoleman.bandcamp.com/track/revealing-the-holy.

I saw Mary in the Garden (suggested for the church service on The call of Mary Magdalene)

I saw Mary in the Garden
walk down
Sun made a rainbow with her tears
The angel said, 'I beg your pardon'
The One you're looking for's not here.

Someone came alive again, oh yes he did.
Someone came alive again, pushed up the lid,
Someone came alive again and I don't kid.
walk down
Just walked out in the sunshine, oh yes he did.

I saw Jesus eating mackerel
When he'd been dead a week before
And Peter looked so strong and thankful
Counting fishes on the shore.

Someone came alive again, oh yes he did.
Someone came alive again, pushed up the lid,
Someone came alive again and I don't kid
walk down
Just walked out in the sunshine, oh yes he did.

And we who live like nothing's different,
Like there's no power in our lives,
Ask God to take the stone and shift it
So that our dying heart revives.

Someone came alive again, oh yes he did.
Someone came alive again, pushed up the lid,
Someone came alive again and I don't kid.
walk down
Just walked out in the sunshine, oh yes he did.

Rowland Howarth © 2012 L'Arche, Ipswich

My Spirit Rejoices in My God (suggested for Small Group Celebration 3: Encouragement)

Refrain: My spirit rejoices in my God
                  My spirit rejoices in my God.

My soul glorifies the Lord,
My spirit rejoices in my God.
You look down on your lowly servant;
And blest by all ages will I be.

Marvels, the Almighty works for me.
Holy, holy is your name.
Your mercy is from age to age,
On those who fear your holy name.

You fill the starving with good things,
And empty the rich you send away.
You watch over Israel, your servant;
Your mercy you never will forget.

Brian Halferty © 1976, 2011, Lyrics adapted from Luke 1.46–54
Music by Brian Halferty

Come to the Circle (suggested for Small Group Celebration 4: Welcome)

Come to the circle, my sisters, my brothers,
Come to the circle, for we are all friends.
We gather together, for we are one body.
We give thanks for the circle, and thanks for our friends.

Welcome to the circle ...... *(Name)*,
It's so good you are here,
To break and share your journey with us,
...... *(Name)*, you're welcome here.

CD *Slow Action of Love*, johncoleman.bandcamp.com/track/come-to-the-circle.

Come now Holy Spirit (suggested for Small Group Celebration 12: Gifts)

Come now Holy Spirit, come now, strong like wind and bright like fire.
Come through us, oh help and guide us, boldly come and make the earth all new.
Come to us O Father of the poor, change to joy what we endure.
Come and bring your peace, your justice and release.
Come breaking down our door.
Spirit come.

Heal our wounds, our strength renew, on our dryness pour your dew.
Wash the stains of guilt away, guide our steps when we would go astray.
Bend our stubborn heart and will, we pray, melt the frozen, warm the chill.
Blessed light divine, within our heart come shine, our inmost being fill.
Spirit come.

Come today and come tomorrow, solace in the midst of sorrow,
Pleasant coolness in the heat, welcome rest when labour is complete.
Where you can't be found, our lives distort, nothing good in deed or thought,
Nothing free from ill, no one can fulfil the need which you have wrought.
Spirit come.

Come now Holy Spirit, come now, strong like wind and bright like fire.
Come through us, oh help and guide us, boldly come and make the earth all new.
Come to us O Mother of the poor, change for joy what we endure.
Come and bring your peace, your justice and release.
Come breaking down our door.
Spirit come. Spirit come. Spirit come. Spirit come.

Appendix 3

Booklist

Accessible books for Bible readings

Berryman, Jerome, 2017, *The Complete Guide to Godly Play*, Vol. 2, Church Publishing New York.

Hartman, Bob and Krisztina Kallai Nagy, 2008, *The Lion Storyteller Bible*, Lion Hudson. The section called 'Sharing stories with a crowd' gives suggestions for helpful participative ways of telling the stories.

NIrV: an accessible New Testament designed to be more accessible to readers with learning disabilities or moderate sight loss. It is in large print, with illustrations and helpful navigation. Order from www.livability.org.uk

Open Praise Project Easy Read Bible Stories aiming to bring Bible stories to life in an accessible and sensory way: https://openpraiseproject.com

Peterson, Eugene H., 2009, *The Message*, NavPress.

Royle, S., 2016, *Easy-to-Read Version* (ERV), World Bible Translation Centre.

Tutu, Desmond, 2010, *Children of God: Storybook Bible*, Zonderkidz.

Vanier, Jean, 1985, *I walk with Jesus*, Paulist Press.

Vanier, Jean, 1987, *I meet Jesus*, Paulist Press.

Resource material from L'Arche and Faith and Light

Faith and Light, *Annual Guidelines*.
   Excellent outlines for small group celebrations. They can be ordered on the Faith and Light International website: www.faithandlight.org/rubriques/haut/publications/faith-and-light-publications

L'Arche Daybreak, 1995, *Living the Beatitudes: Daily Reflections for Lent From the L'Arche Daybreak Community*, St Anthony Messenger Press.
   Short true stories from daily life in L'Arche with a reflection on each one and suggestions for prayer.

Procter, Andrew, 2005, *A Month Among the Vines: Daily devotions based on time shared with a L'Arche community in France*, Redemptorist Publications.
   True stories from daily life in L'Arche with a reflection on each one.

Wilson, Hilary, 2004, *My life together: L'Arche Communities and the Challenge of Unity*, Darton, Longman and Todd.

Resource books from outside L'Arche

JUST Teaching Books 1–4: Causeway, Prospects, Scripture Union.
A series of Bible Daily Notes (books or CDs) on various biblical themes, e.g. 'God gives new life'. There is a short easy-to-read Bible reading, an explanation of it, and a suggested simple prayer for each day in a month – all on one small page.

Mental Health Foundation, 2004, *What is important to you? A booklet for people with learning disabilities.*
Why are we here? – Spirituality and the lives of people with learning disabilities, Updates, 020 7802 0300, www.mentalhealth.org.uk

Swinton, John, 2001, *A Space to Listen: Meeting the spiritual needs of people with learning disabilities*, Foundation for People with learning disabilities, www.learningdisabilities.org.uk

Books with creative ideas

Brind, Jan and Tessa Wilkinson, 2008, *Creative Ideas for Evening Prayer: For Seasons, Feasts and Special Occasions Throughout the Year – An All-Age Resource,* Canterbury Press.

Brind, Jan and Tessa Wilkinson 2009, *Crafts for Creative Worship: Ideas for Enriching All-age Worship Through the Year*, Canterbury Press.

Wider reading

Hollins, Sheila, and John Swinton and Katie Carpenter, 2018, *Going to Church*, Books Beyond Words.

Melcher, Sarah and Mikeal Parsons, Amos Yong (eds), 2018, *The Bible and Disability, a Commentary*, SCM Press.

Pailin, David, 1992, *A Gentle Touch: From a theology of handicap to a theology of human being*, SPCK.

Reynolds, Thomas E., 2008, *Vulnerable Communion: A Theology of Disability and Hospitality*, Brazos Press.

Swinton, John, 2004, *Critical Reflections on Stanley Hauerwas' Theology of Disability – Disabling Society, Enabling Theology*, The Haworth Pastoral Press.

Tupling, Katie and Anna de Lange, 2018, *Worship and Disability*, Grove Books.

Young, Frances, 1997, *Encounter with Mystery – Reflections on L'Arche and living with disability*, Darton, Longman and Todd.

Appendix 4

Online resources

Organizations for People with Disabilities

Caritas St. Joseph's: www.stjoseph.org.uk/caritas. Training on working with people with learning disabilities through their 'Symbols of Faith' course. They also give support and advice on liturgies for Inclusive Masses.

Churches For All: A network of UK Christian disability organizations with links to partner organizations: www.churchesforall.org.uk.

Enabling Church: www.churchesforall.org.uk/EnablingChurch.

Faith and Light communities in England, Scotland or Wales: www.faithandlight. org.uk.

Faith and Light communities in Ireland and Northern Ireland: www.faithandlight. ie.

Inclusive Church: www.inclusive-church.org/disability.

L'Arche International: www.larche.org.

L'Arche UK: www.larche.org.uk.

Livability: www.livability.org.uk. Supports church groups working for accessible church. Groups may be called Prospects, Causeway, or have their own chosen name. They hold accessible and inclusive church training days and provide teaching and worship materials.

Through the Roof: www.throughtheroof.org. Equips churches and the Christian community to fully involve people with disabilities.

Do contact your local Anglican or Roman Catholic diocesan disability advisor or the relevant person in other churches.

Signing

Makaton: www.makaton.org.

Picture Exchange Communication System: www.pecs-unitedkingdom.com/pecs.

Signalong: www.signalong.org.uk.

Other resources

An online Bible with good search facilities and many translations of the Bible:
   www.biblegateway.com/.
Godly Play: www.godlyplayfoundation.org.
Godly Play UK: www.godlyplay.uk.
Godly Play trainers can be invited to your church to introduce Godly Play.
www.buildfaith.org/lent-in-a-bag.

Appendix 5

Templates

The templates may be downloaded for free in A4 size from the Canterbury Press website, at www.canterburypress.co.uk.

Page 77: The Feeding of the 5,000

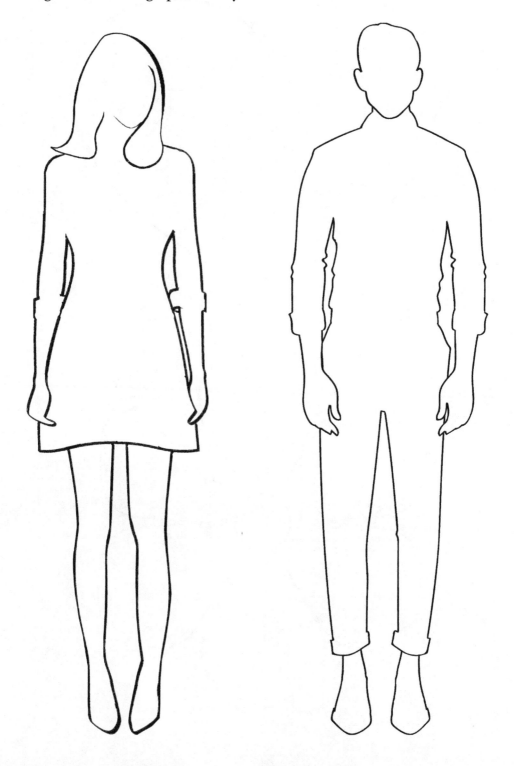

Page 135: Forgiveness and Reconciliation

Page 161: Transformation

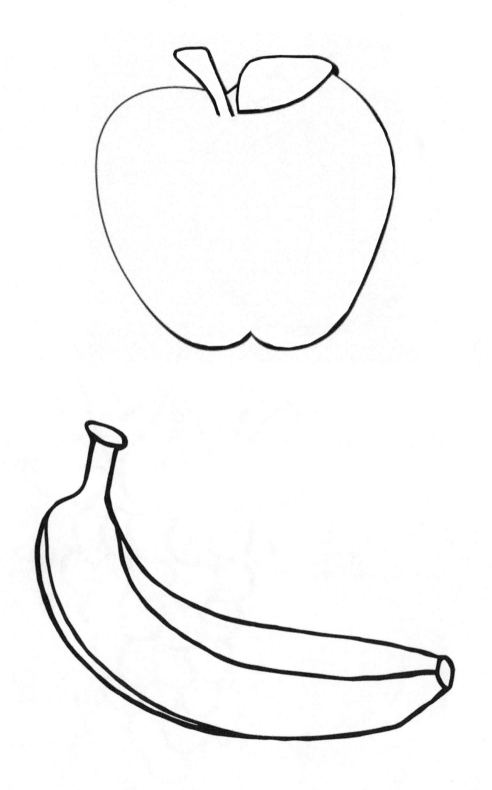

Notes

1 L'Arche Daybreak Community, 1995, *Living the Beatitudes: Daily Reflections for Lent*, St Anthony Messenger Press, p. 35.

2 Jean Vanier and John Swinton, 2014, *Mental Health, The Inclusive Church Resource*, Darton, Longman and Todd, pp. 100–1.

3 Frances Young, 1990, *Face to Face: Narrative Essay in the Theology of Suffering*, Clark, Edinburgh, p. 137.

4 Jean Vanier, 2006, *Community and Growth*, revised edition, Darton, Longman and Todd, p. 174.

5 www.youtube.com/watch?v=pct_yxXwHfY.

CPSIA information can be obtained
at www.ICGtesting.com
Printed in the USA
BVHW060817130819
555729BV00017B/279/P